Math Expressions

Homework and Remembering • Volume 1

Developed by
The Children's Math Worlds Research Project

PROJECT DIRECTOR AND AUTHOR
Dr. Karen C. Fuson

This material is based upon work supported by the
National Science Foundation
under Grant Numbers
ESI-9816320, REC-9806020, and RED-935373.

Any opinions, findings, and conclusions, or recommendations expressed in this material
are those of the author and do not necessarily reflect the views of the National Science Foundation.

Teacher Reviewers

Kindergarten
Patricia Stroh Sugiyama
Wilmette, Illinois

Barbara Wahle
Evanston, Illinois

Grade 1
Sandra Budson
Newton, Massachusetts

Janet Pecci
Chicago, Illinois

Megan Rees
Chicago, Illinois

Grade 2
Molly Dunn
Danvers, Massachusetts

Agnes Lesnick
Hillside, Illinois

Rita Soto
Chicago, Illinois

Grade 3
Jane Curran
Honesdale, Pennsylvania

Sandra Tucker
Chicago, Illinois

Grade 4
Sara Stoneberg Llibre
Chicago, Illinois

Sheri Roedel
Chicago, Illinois

Grade 5
Todd Atler
Chicago, Illinois

Leah Barry
Norfolk, Massachusetts

Credits

Cover art: © Arco Images GmbH/Alamy
Illustrative art: Dave Klug
Technical art: Morgan-Cain & Associates

Name _______________________   Date _______________________

Homework

Solve for the unknown number.

1. 3 × 7 = _______

2. 32 / 4 = _______

3. 7 × 5 = _______

4. 6 × _______ = 24

5. 5 × _______ = 30

6. 3 × _______ = 24

7. 15 / 3 = _______

8. 20 / 5 = _______

9. 18 / 6 = _______

10. 9 • 2 = _______

11. 3 • 9 = _______

12. 4 • 4 = _______

Write an equation for each word problem and then solve the problem.

Show your work.

13. There are 4 measuring cups in a set. Mr. Merton's science class has 7 sets of measuring cups. How many cups are there altogether? _______________________

14. A carousel has 40 horses. There are 4 horses in each row. How many rows are there on the carousel? _______________________

15. Morgan has 24 dollars. She wants to buy party hats that cost 3 dollars each. How many party hats can Morgan buy? _______________________

16. The Garcias have a grandfather clock that needs to be wound once a week. How many times will they need to wind it during the month of February, which has 28 days? _______________________

17. There are 8 cars in a repair shop. All 8 cars need 4 new tires. How many tires will be needed in all? _______________________

18. Write a multiplication or division word problem of your own. Then write an equation and solve the problem.

____

____

____

Remembering

Complete.

1. $2 \times \underline{\hspace{1cm}} = 6$

2. $10 / 5 = \underline{\hspace{1cm}}$

3. $\underline{\hspace{1cm}} \times 3 = 12$

4. $\underline{\hspace{1cm}} \times 5 = 25$

5. $6 \cdot \underline{\hspace{1cm}} = 24$

6. $7 \times 2 = \underline{\hspace{1cm}}$

7. $16 / 8 = \underline{\hspace{1cm}}$

8. $\underline{\hspace{1cm}} \times 1 = 9$

9. $\underline{\hspace{1cm}} \cdot 4 = 20$

10. $3 \times \underline{\hspace{1cm}} = 18$

11. $\underline{\hspace{1cm}} \times 7 = 28$

12. $9 / 3 = \underline{\hspace{1cm}}$

13. $4 \times 10 = \underline{\hspace{1cm}}$

14. $2 \cdot \underline{\hspace{1cm}} = 4$

15. $\underline{\hspace{1cm}} \times 6 = 6$

Write an equation. Then solve the problem.

16. Tanya plans to read 2 books each month. If she achieves her goal, how many books will she read in one year?

17. To prepare for a math test, Elena studied for one and one-half hours. For how many minutes did Elena study?

18. Anthony wants to distribute 15 toys equally to each of his 5 friends. How many toys should each friend receive?

19. Kelvin's birthday is 14 days from today. How many weeks will it be until Kelvin celebrates his birthday?

20. A kennel is caring for 5 pets. Last week, the kennel cared for 3 times as many pets. How many pets did the kennel care for last week?

21. An egg carton has spaces for one dozen eggs. If there are 2 rows of 4 eggs in the carton, how many spaces in the carton are empty?

FP–2

Homework

**Name the kind of situation shown, and write an equation.
Then solve each problem.**

1. A large box of crayons holds
60 crayons. There are 10 crayons in
each row. How many rows are there?

Situation: ________________

Equation: ________________

____

2. A poster is 4 feet long by 3 feet
wide. How many square feet of
wall space will it cover?

Situation: ________________

Equation: ________________

____

3. A bingo card has 5 rows and
5 columns of squares. Jasmine and
her friend need every square covered
to win. How many squares must be
covered to win the game?

Situation: ________________

Equation: ________________

____

4. There are 28 students in
Mrs. Fletcher's class. She has
divided them into 7 groups for a
science project. How many students
are there in each group?

Situation: ________________

Equation: ________________

____

Find the unknown length (l), width (w), or area (A). Remember: $A = l \times w$.

5. $6 \times 3 = A$

$A =$ ________

6. $8 \times w = 32$

$w =$ ________

7. $A = 7 \cdot 5$

$A =$ ________

8. $45 / 5 = l$

$l =$ ________

9.

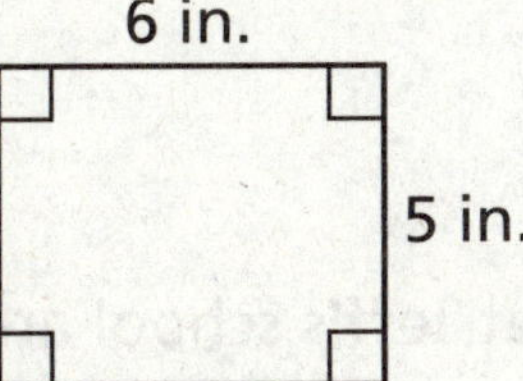

Area = ________ sq in.

10.

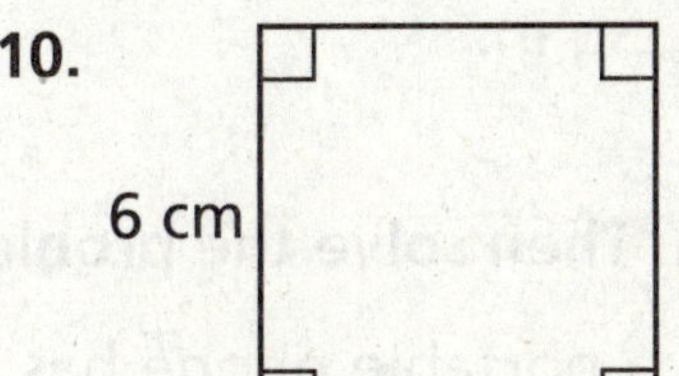

length = ________ cm

11. A rectangle has an area of 18 square meters. The length and
width are whole numbers. Write all the possible lengths and
widths for this rectangle.

____

____

Name _______________________ **Date** _______________________

Remembering

Complete.

1. $3 \times 3 =$ _______

2. $10 \times$ _______ $= 20$

3. _______ $\times 5 = 30$

4. _______ $\times 7 = 21$

5. $24 / 6 =$ _______

6. $1 \times$ _______ $= 11$

7. $4 \times 8 =$ _______

8. $9 \times$ _______ $= 36$

9. _______ $\times 8 = 72$

Find the unknown Length.

10. $7 \cdot w = 42$
$w =$ _______

11. $A = 6 \cdot 8$
$A =$ _______

12. $l \cdot 6 = 18$
$l =$ _______

13. $9 \times 9 = A$
$A =$ _______

14. $27 = 3 \cdot w$
$w =$ _______

15. $l \times 4 = 24$
$l =$ _______

16. $2 \times w = 14$
$w =$ _______

17. $63 = l \cdot 9$
$l =$ _______

18. $40 = 4 \cdot w$
$w =$ _______

Write the missing measurement.

19. 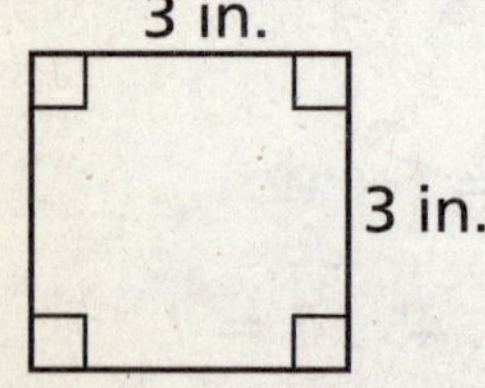

Area = _______ sq in.

20. 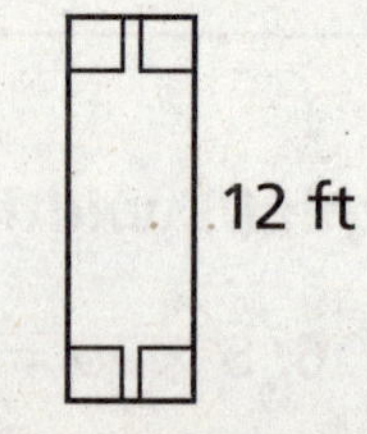

Area = 24 sq ft

width = _______ ft

Write an equation. Then solve the problem.

21. On its keypad, a portable phone has 21 buttons, and there are 3 buttons in each row. How many rows of buttons are on the keypad?

Equation _______________________

____

22. Twenty people at Jeff's school are going on a field trip. If 5 people can ride in each car, how many cars are needed for the field trip?

Equation _______________________

____

Homework

Write the situation: equal groups, array, or area. Then write an equation and solve the problem.

1. In the Cozy Cafe there are 6 chairs at each table. Altogether, there are 42 chairs. How many tables are there at the Cozy Cafe?

   Situation: _______________

   Equation: _______________

   ____

2. Hester measured the patio in her backyard. It is 10 feet long and 9 feet wide. How many square feet of ground does it cover?

   Situation: _______________

   Equation: _______________

   ____

3. Miguel visited an apple orchard. He saw 8 rows and 6 columns of trees. How many apple trees are there in all?

   Situation: _______________

   Equation: _______________

   ____

4. The movie theater in Cloverville has 72 seats arranged in 9 rows. How many seats are in each row?

   Situation: _______________

   Equation: _______________

   ____

Find the unknown area (A), length (l), or width (w) in each equation.

5. $9 \times 7 = A$

   $A =$ _______

6. $l = 81 \div 9$

   $l =$ _______

7. $6 \cdot 7 = A$

   $A =$ _______

8. $64 \div 8 = w$

   $w =$ _______

9. $5 \times l = 35$

   $l =$ _______

10. $27 / 9 = w$

    $w =$ _______

11. $40 = 5 \times l$

    $l =$ _______

12. $4 \times l = 36$

    $l =$ _______

13. $56 \div w = 8$

    $w =$ _______

14. $A = 8 \times 6$

    $A =$ _______

15. $45 = l \times 5$

    $l =$ _______

16. $25 \cdot w = 100$

    $w =$ _______

Answer each question.

17. If $8 \times 12 = 96$, then what is 12×8? _______

18. If $144 \div 9 = 16$, then what is 16×9? _______

Remembering

Multiply or divide.

1. 8 • 9 = _______   2. 7 • 7 = _______   3. 4 • 2 = _______

4. 99 ÷ 9 = _______   5. 16 / 4 = _______   6. 56 ÷ 8 = _______

7. 9 × 9 = _______   8. 63 ÷ 7 = _______   9. 3 × 7 = _______

10. 20 / 4 = _______   11. 5 × 5 = _______   12. 13 × _______ = 13

13. 9 • 5 = _______   14. 27 ÷ 9 = _______   15. 10 • 10 = _______

16. 8 / 8 = _______   17. $\frac{18}{9}$ = _______   18. $\frac{80}{8}$ = _______

Write each quotient.

19. $2\overline{)20}$ 20. $6\overline{)30}$ 21. $7\overline{)63}$ 22. $8\overline{)24}$ 23. $5\overline{)0}$

24. $5\overline{)15}$ 25. $4\overline{)24}$ 26. $9\overline{)36}$ 27. $3\overline{)9}$ 28. $4\overline{)28}$

Solve.

29. Aimee invited 5 friends to her birthday party. If Aimee and
her friends will sit in equal numbers at 2 tables, how many
people will be seated at each table?

____

30. A quilt is made of 8 rows of squares, and there are 6 squares
in each row. Each square measures 1 foot on a side. Explain
how to find the area of the quilt in square feet. Then write
the area.

____

____

____

____

Homework

Complete.

1. $9 \times$ _______ $= 36$ 2. $81 \div 9 =$ _______   3. $1 \cdot$ _______ $= 26$

4. _______ $\times 5 = 25$ 5. $32 \div 4 =$ _______   6. $0 \times 9 =$ _______

7. $0 \div 16 =$ _______   8. $14 \cdot$ _______ $= 0$ 9. _______ $\times 10 = 10$

10. $49 \div 7 =$ _______   11. $4 \cdot$ _______ $= 28$ 12. $40 \div 8 =$ _______

For each problem, tell what kind of situation is described. Then write an equation and solve.

13. A marching band volunteers to paint a mural. The mural covers an area of 15 square feet. If the mural is 5 feet wide, what is its length?

Situation: _______________________

Equation: _______________________

____

14. The marching-band director orders 10 packages of music books. Each package has 8 music books. How many music books will she receive?

Situation: _______________________

Equation: _______________________

____

15. Each drummer has 4 drumsticks, making a total of 36 drumsticks. How many drummers are in the band?

Situation: _______________________

Equation: _______________________

____

16. The band has 48 people. There are 6 people in each row. How many rows are there in the marching band?

Situation: _______________________

Equation: _______________________

____

Which of these answers cannot be right? How do you know?

17. $32 \times 14 = 448$ $53 \times 17 = 906$ $46 \times 18 = 828$

____

____

____

____

Name   Date

Remembering

Solve for the unknown.

1. $72 \div \underline{\quad} = 8$

2. $\frac{32}{8} = \underline{\quad}$

3. $\underline{\quad} \div 8 = 6$

4. $5 \times \underline{\quad} = 30$

5. $7 = \underline{\quad} \div 6$

6. $\underline{\quad} = 8 \times 8$

7. $\underline{\quad} = 35 \div 5$

8. $7 \times \underline{\quad} = 56$

9. $\underline{\quad} \times 10 = 100$

10. $\underline{\quad} = 24 \div 6$

11. $3 \times \underline{\quad} = 0$

12. $20 \div \underline{\quad} = 5$

13. $27 = 9 \times \underline{\quad}$

14. $\underline{\quad} = 2 \times 8$

15. $6 = \underline{\quad} \div 2$

16. $\underline{\quad} \times 4 = 40$

17. $3 = 6 \div \underline{\quad}$

18. $\underline{\quad} \times 8 = 0$

19. $9 \times \underline{\quad} = 45$

20. $\underline{\quad} = 36 \div 6$

21. $54 = \underline{\quad} \times 6$

22. $15 - 6 = \underline{\quad}$

23. $12 - 12 = 1 \times \underline{\quad}$

24. $7 \times \underline{\quad} = 8 + 6$

Solve.

25. The attendance for 2 performances of a school play was 361 people in total. If 193 people attended the first performance, how many attended the second?

26. The school purchased 63 new computers. An equal number of these new computers were given to 9 classes. How many new computers did each class receive?

27. A classroom contains 4 rows of desks. There are 7 desks in each row. How many desks does the classroom contain?

28. A bulletin board has a length of 7 feet. The width is 3 feet. What is the area of the wall covered by the bulletin board?

29. During the first lunch period of the day, 48 students sit in equal groups at each of 8 cafeteria tables. What number of students sit at each table?

30. The students sit in 5 rows in the auditorium. If 40 students are equally seated in the rows, how many students sit in each row?

Homework

Solve each word problem. Label your answer.

1. Maria created artwork by placing all of her seashells in 4 rows on a wall. In each row, she arranged 8 seashells. How many seashells did Maria collect in all?

   ____

2. Arturo collected 18 seashells. He wants to divide the seashells evenly among his 3 best friends. How many seashells will each friend receive?

   ____

Use the pictograph and key to solve.

Katie planted pumpkins in the spring. Now she is selling them This pictograph shows how many pumpkins she sold this weekend.

Friday	🎃 🎃 🎃 🎃
Saturday	🎃 🎃 🎃 🎃 🎃 🎃 🎃
Sunday	🎃 🎃 🎃

Key: 🎃 = 6 pumpkins

3. How many pumpkins did Katie sell this weekend?

   ____

4. How many more pumpkins did she sell on Saturday than on Friday?

   ____

5. On Sunday Katie sold the pumpkins for $3.00 each or 2 for $5.00. What is the least amount of money she could have taken in?

   ____

6. On Friday Katie sold half the pumpkins for $3.00 each and the rest at 2 for $5.00. How much money did she take in on Friday?

   ____

Remembering

Dear Math Student,

I am giving a party tomorrow, and I invited 10 people to come. I bought 10 party bags and planned to put 8 marbles in each bag. Now I hear that my two cousins will be in town, so there will be 12 people altogether.

How many marbles will I need to buy? I don't know how to multiply 12×8. It is not part of my multiplication table.

Please send me a letter explaining how to figure this out. Thank you.

Sincerely,

Puzzled Penguin

____

____

____

____

____

____

____

____

____

Will the following products be even or odd? How do you know?

1. 57×57 _______________   2. 82×96 _______________

3. 91×23 _______________   4. 76×75 _______________

5. 27×81 _______________   6. 92×20 _______________

7. 45×55 _______________   8. 31×31 _______________

9. 73×84 _______________   10. 52×32 _______________

Name ___________________   **Date** ___________________

Homework

Complete.

1. $6 \times 3 =$ _______   2. $7 \times 9 =$ _______   3. $4 \times 0 =$ _______

4. $30 \div 5$ _______   5. $18 \div 2 =$ _______   6. $70 \div 7 =$ _______

7. $36 \div$ _______ $= 9$ 8. $3 \times$ _______ $= 24$ 9. _______ $\div 8 = 0$

10. _______ $\times 7 = 35$ 11. $60 =$ _______ $\times 6$ 12. $4 = 28 \div$ _______

13. $72 = 8 \times$ _______   14. $2 =$ _______ $\div 10$ 15. _______ $= 45 \div 9$

16. $21 =$ _______ $\times 7$ 17. $8 = 64 \div$ _______   18. _______ $\times 374 = 0$

Solve.

19. Using only whole numbers, Nikki wrote as many multiplication equations as she could with 12 as the product. What were her equations?

____

____

20. Pablo wrote four division equations with 6 as the quotient. What could have been the four division equations that he wrote?

____

____

For each problem, tell what kind of situation is described. Then write an equation and solve.

21. Each student gathered 10 leaves for the group art project. The group collected a total of 80 leaves. How many students are in the group?

Situation: ___________________________

Equation: ___________________________

____

22. The display had storage boxes in stacked rows. Each row had 7 boxes. If a total of 42 boxes were used, how many rows were in the display?

Situation: ___________________________

Equation: ___________________________

____

Name ___________________________ Date ___________________

Remembering

Complete.

1. $5 \times$ _______ $= 0$

2. $1 \times$ _______ $= 28$

3. $6 \times$ _______ $= 36$

4. $63 \div 9 =$ _______

5. _______ $\times 7 = 56$

6. $8 \times$ _______ $= 24$

7. $50 \div$ _______ $= 10$

8. $6 \times$ _______ $= 12$

9. $\dfrac{54}{9} =$ _______

10. $24 \div$ _______ $= 6$

11. _______ $\div 8 = 9$

12. _______ $\times 4 = 16$

13. $5 \times$ _______ $= 40$

14. $35 \div 7 =$ _______

15. _______ $\div 6 = 8$

16. $9 \times 7 =$ _______

17. _______ $\div 11 = 1$

18. _______ $= 64 \div 8$

22. _______ $\div 15 = 0$

23. $16 \times$ _______ $= 0$

24. $12 \times$ _______ $= 24$

Complete.

25. If $10 \times 25 = 250$, then what is $250 \div 10$? _______

26. If $144 \div 24 = 6$, then what is 6×24? _______

27. If $15 \times 15 = 225$, then what is $225 \div 15$? _______

28. If $156 \div 13 = 12$, then what is $156 \div 12$? _______

29. If $288 \div 18 = 16$, then what is 18×16? _______

30. If $9 \times 45 = 405$, then what is $405 \div 45$? _______

Solve.

31. Tom found that the product of 14×3 is 12. Is this product correct? If not, explain how to find the correct product.

____

____

32. Katrina has 20 photographs to arrange in an array in the school's yearbook. How many different ways can she arrange the photographs? Explain how you found your answers.

____

____

____

     Multiplication and Division Practice

Name _______________ **Date** _______________

Homework

**Write the situation: equal groups, array, area, or combination.
Then write an equation and solve the problem.**

1. A chessboard has 8 rows of squares. There are 64 squares total. How many columns are on a chessboard?

Situation: _______________

Equation: _______________

____

2. A sandbox is 9 feet long and 6 feet wide. How many square feet of ground does the sandbox cover?

Situation: _______________

Equation: _______________

____

3. The Ferris wheel in Paradise Park has 10 seats. Each seat can hold 3 people. How many people can ride the Ferris wheel at the same time?

Situation: _______________

Equation: _______________

____

4. Dan makes invitations out of red, white, and blue paper. Each has a star or a flag pattern. How many kinds of invitations can he make?

Situation: _______________

Equation: _______________

____

5. Mr. Caruso is a builder who always builds the same kind of house. Only the materials are different. How many different houses can Mr. Caruso build?

Situation: _______________

Equation: _______________

____

Red Brick	Tile Roof
Brown Brick	Slate Roof
Yellow Brick	Cedar Roof

Find the unknown number in each equation.

6. $a = 6 \times 7$

$a =$ _______

7. $b = 81 \div 9$

$b =$ _______

8. $5 \cdot 8 = c$

$c =$ _______

9. $7e = 21$

$e =$ _______

10. $10f = 50$

$f =$ _______

11. $42 \div 6 = g$

$g =$ _______

12. $72 = 9k$

$k =$ _______

13. $54 = 9p$

$p =$ _______

Practice multiplications and divisions with your Target.

Remembering

Complete.

1. $11 \times$ _______ $= 88$
2. _______ $\div 12 = 1$
3. $6 \times 8 =$ _______

4. _______ $\div 2 = 5$
5. $5 \times$ _______ $= 45$
6. _______ $\div 6 = 9$

7. $2 \times 3 =$ _______
8. _______ $\times 5 = 35$
9. $4 \times$ _______ $= 16$

10. _______ $\div 7 = 7$
11. $20 \div 4 =$ _______
12. $35 \div 7 =$ _______

13. $2 \times$ _______ $= 16$
14. _______ $\div 3 = 9$
15. _______ $\times 4 = 36$

16. _______ $\times 6 = 36$
17. $4 \times$ _______ $= 0$
18. $63 \div 7 =$ _______

Write each quotient.

19. $8\overline{)32}$
20. $7\overline{)14}$
21. $3\overline{)30}$
22. $5\overline{)25}$
23. $9\overline{)81}$

Solve for the unknown.

24. $18 \div l = 6$

   $l =$ _______

25. $8w = 72$

   $w =$ _______

26. $1 \cdot 10 = A$

   $A =$ _______

27. $\frac{12}{w} = 6$

   $w =$ _______

28. $9 * 3 = A$

   $A =$ _______

29. $\frac{l}{7} = 3$

   $l =$ _______

Write an equation and use it to solve the problem.

30. A café lunch menu offers a choice of a sandwich or salad, and
    four types of soup. Find the number of different combinations
    of a sandwich or salad, and a soup. Explain your answer.

    ____

    ____

    ____

    ____

   Make Combinations

Homework

The graph below shows the number of planes arriving in River City today.

1. There were ________ times as many planes in the morning as in the afternoon.

2. There were ________ as many planes in the afternoon as in the morning.

Tell what situation is shown, write an equation, and solve the problem.

3. Amanda has 63 bracelets. She decides to divide the bracelets equally among 7 friends. How many bracelets does she give each friend?

Situation: ____________________

Equation: ____________________

____

4. Mr. Gordon is planting a garden. He plans to make his garden 12 feet by 3 feet. How many square feet will his garden be?

Situation: ____________________

Equation: ____________________

____

Find the unknown number in each equation.

5. $8a = 56$

$a =$ ______

6. $b = 63 \div 9$

$b =$ ______

7. $5 \cdot 6 = c$

$c =$ ______

8. $6d = 54$

$d =$ ______

9. $49 \div 7 = e$

$e =$ ______

10. $7f = 63$

$f =$ ______

11. $5g = 45$

$g =$ ______

12. $64 = 8h$

$h =$ ______

13. $36 / 6 = j$

$j =$ ______

Use your Target to practice multiplications and divisions.

Remembering

Solve for the unknown.

1. $7 = 56 \div k$

$k =$ ______

2. $4 = 28 / y$

$y =$ ______

3. $10 \times c = 50$

$c =$ ______

4. $24 = 3r$

$r =$ ______

5. $6q = 54$

$q =$ ______

6. $m / 8 = 6$

$m =$ ______

7. $5 = s \div 9$

$s =$ ______

8. $6 \times 6 = b$

$b =$ ______

9. $40 \div g = 5$

$g =$ ______

Write an equation and use it to solve the problem.

10. This summer, it has rained only $\frac{1}{4}$ as much as last summer. Last summer, 12 inches of rain fell. What amount of rain has fallen this summer?

Equation: ________________________

____

11. Clarice is $\frac{1}{5}$ as old as her mother, and twice as old as her brother Jason. Clarice's mother is 30 years old. How old is Jason?

Equation: ________________________

____

The graph below shows the number of books that a student in Mrs. Jacobsen's class read during April and May.

Complete each statement.

12. There were ______ times as many books read during May as during April.

13. There were ______ as many books read during April as during May.

  Understand Comparisons

Homework

Name ______________________ **Date** ______________________

Solve for the unknown.

1. $5 \cdot 6 = a$

   $a = $ ______

2. $b = 64 \div 8$

   $b = $ ______

3. $c = 7 \times 8$

   $c = $ ______

4. $40 \div 5 = d$

   $d = $ ______

5. $7e = 49$

   $e = $ ______

6. $50 \cdot f = 100$

   $f = $ ______

7. $54 \div 9 = g$

   $g = $ ______

8. $4h = 28$

   $h = $ ______

9. $45 = 5k$

   $k = $ ______

10. $6l = 36$

    $l = $ ______

11. $9n = 0$

    $n = $ ______

12. $72 = 8p$

    $p = $ ______

Identify the kind of situation and write an equation. Then solve the problem.

13. Isabel earned 42 dollars mowing lawns last month. Her sister earned only $\frac{1}{6}$ as much. How much money did Isabel's sister earn?

    Situation: ______________________

    Equation: ______________________

    ____

14. Daniel packed black, tan, and blue shorts in his suitcase. He also packed 6 different T-shirts. How many different outfits will Daniel have?

    Situation: ______________________

    Equation: ______________________

    ____

15. A large muffin tray holds 5 muffins across and 7 muffins down. How many muffins can the tray hold?

    Situation: ______________________

    Equation: ______________________

    ____

16. The Richardson family has a tent that covers 54 square feet of ground. It is 9 feet long. How wide is the tent?

    Situation: ______________________

    Equation: ______________________

    ____

17. Farmer O'Malley bought new horseshoes for all of his horses today. He bought 36 horseshoes. How many horses does Farmer O'Malley have?

    Situation: ______________________

    Equation: ______________________

    ____

18. Mrs. Pinckett planted 8 rose bushes in her garden. She planted 3 times as many azalea bushes. How many azalea bushes did she plant?

    Situation: ______________________

    Equation: ______________________

    ____

Practice multiplications and divisions with your Target.

Remembering

Solve for the unknown.

1. $x = 42 \div 7$

$x = $ _______

2. $10 \times y = 50$

$y = $ _______

3. $5c = 45$

$c = $ _______

4. $t \times 2 = 0$

$t = $ _______

5. $n \div 8 = 9$

$n = $ _______

6. $7 \times 8 = q$

$q = $ _______

7. $\frac{r}{9} = 7$

$r = $ _______

8. $\frac{48}{6} = w$

$w = $ _______

9. $\frac{36}{f} = 4$

$f = $ _______

10. $4h = 31 - 3$

$h = $ _______

11. $k = 27 \div 3$

$k = $ _______

12. $16 - 9 = z$

$z = $ _______

13. $s \div 6 = 8$

$s = $ _______

14. $45 \div b = 5$

$b = $ _______

15. $e = 32 \div 8$

$e = $ _______

Write an equation. Then use the equation to solve the problem.

16. When deciding what to wear, a student must choose from 2 pairs of jeans and 5 T-shirts. How many different combinations of one pair of jeans and one T-shirt can be made?

____

17. One section of a theater contains 6 rows of seats. Each row has the same number of seats. Altogether, 54 people can sit in the seats. How many seats are in each row in that section of the theater?

____

18. The number of basketball coaches in a league is $\frac{1}{7}$ the number of players. How many coaches are at the school if 63 players are in the league?

____

19. At a figure skating performance, $\frac{1}{3}$ of the skaters completed a triple jump. If 18 skaters performed, how many skaters did not complete a triple jump?

____

  Practice with Multiplication Problems

Name   **Date**

Homework

1. Write the next two numbers in this sequence:

   9 18 27 36 45 _______ _______

2. If you multiply 67 × 67, will your answer be even or odd?
   _______ How do you know? _____________________

3. If 35 × 25 is 875, then what is 875 ÷ 25? _______

4. What is *n* in this equation: 18 × 3 = 9 × *n*? _______

5. What is *n* in this equation: 7 × 6 = 5 × 6 + *n* × 6? _______

6. If one person counts by 3 to 60 and another person counts
   by 6 to 60, will any of those numbers be the same? Explain.

   ____

   ____

   ____

7. Complete the Scrambled
   Multiplication Table.

×										
	20					70				
	14			63	21	49		28		35
			80				64		48	
				81	27				54	
	8				12	28				20
		1		9						
					9			12	18	
			60		18	42			36	
		5		45			40			
			20	18				8		10

Solve.

8. At the dog show there are 56 retrievers.
   There are only $\frac{1}{8}$ as many collies. How
   many collies are at the show?

   ____

9. A small track has 9 rows of bleachers.
   Each row holds 8 people. How many
   people can sit in the bleachers?

   ____

Remembering

Complete the Scrambled Multiplication Table.

1.

×										
	12						36			
				56						64
		36						30		
	6				20				4	
		30					45			
			21	30				15		
	27					36				72
			10			40			20	
					10				2	
	21		7							

Write an equation and solve the problem.

2. Zachary's birthday is 9 weeks from today. In how many days will Zachary be celebrating his birthday?

____

3. A school bus can carry 40 passengers seated in rows of 4. How many rows of seats are in the bus?

____

4. A board game is shaped like a square array and is made up of 36 squares. How many rows and how many columns are in the array?

____

5. In a middle school fifth-grade class, there are 5 girls for every 4 boys. Altogether, the class has 27 students. How many boys are in the class?

____

6. On a separate sheet of paper, write an equal-groups problem and an area problem. Make one be a division problem.

Write Word Problems

Name _______________________ **Date** _______________

Homework

For each table, write the rule and complete the table. Then write an equation.

1.

Rule:	
Input	**Output**
0	
4	2
8	
12	6
16	

2.

Rule:	
Input	**Output**
6	1
9	
11	
14	9
8	

Equation: _______________

Equation: _______________

For each table, write a rule using words and an equation with two variables. Then complete the table.

3.

Rule in Words					
Equation					
Hours (h)	1		3		5
Distance in miles (d)	4	8		16	20

4.

Rule in Words					
Equation					
Number of insects (i)		2	3	4	5
Number of legs (l)	6	12	18		

5.

Rule in Words						
Equation						
Number of trees (t)	1	2	3	5	8	10
Number of shrubs (s)	4	8			32	36

6.

Rule in Words						
Equation						
Sue's age (s)	5	10	14	17		27
Ted's age (t)	3	8			17	25

Remembering

Solve for the unknown.

1. $q = \frac{56}{8}$

   $q =$ _______

2. $5 = \frac{20}{r}$

   $r =$ _______

3. $\frac{v}{9} = 8$

   $v =$ _______

4. $6c = 36$

   $c =$ _______

5. $9s = 63$

   $s =$ _______

6. $45 = a \times 5$

   $a =$ _______

7. $2g = 8$

   $g =$ _______

8. $n = 49 \div 7$

   $n =$ _______

9. $9 \times 8 = u$

   $u =$ _______

Solve.

10. $8 \times 0 =$ _______

11. $1 \times 12 =$ _______

12. $9 \times 1 =$ _______

13. $0 \div 6 =$ _______

14. $1 \times 19 =$ _______

15. $0 \div 45 =$ _______

16. $64 \times 1 =$ _______

17. $0 \times 82 =$ _______

18. $0 \div 27 =$ _______

Identify the type of situation and write an equation. Then solve the problem.

19. Each row of a display contains 4 vases. The display contains 24 vases altogether. How many rows of vases are in the display?

    Situation: ____________________

    Equation: ____________________

    ____

20. Marco has 8 red T-shirts and $\frac{1}{4}$ as many blue T-shirts as red T-shirts. How many blue T-shirts does Marco have?

    Situation: ____________________

    Equation: ____________________

    ____

Solve.

21. This winter, 36 inches of snow fell. Last winter, only $\frac{1}{3}$ as much snow fell. How many more inches of snow fell this winter compared to last winter?

    ____

22. In a class of 18 students at Woodworth School, there are $\frac{1}{2}$ as many girls as boys. How many girls are in the class? How many boys?

    ____

Functions

Homework

Find the unknown number in each equation.

1. $p = 3 + (4 \times 5)$ _______

2. $4t + 1 = 25$ _______

3. $5 \times (6 + 3) = m$ _______

4. $6r - 3 = 15$ _______

5. $(12 - 8) \times 7 = b$ _______

6. $n = 16 - (3 \times 4)$ _______

7. $9s = 17 + 1$ _______

8. $5 + (8 \times 6) = c$ _______

9. $7d + 5 = 26$ _______

10. $(6 \times 5) - (4 \times 5) = h$ _______

Write an equation. Then solve the problem.   *Show your work.*

1. Mr. Corelli made a tray of cookies that held 5 across and 7 down. There are 38 students in Mr. Corelli's class. How many more cookies does he need if each student is to get one cookie?

Equation: _____________________

____

2. Leah bought 2 boxes of cookies. She ate 3 cookies and found that she had 21 left. How many cookies were in each box?

Equation: _____________________

____

3. Arturo built 3 sandcastles with 6 towers each. Paco built 5 sandcastles with 4 towers each. Who built more towers? How many more?

Equation: _____________________

____

4. Ashley has 35 dollars. She wants to buy 4 bags of peanuts at 2 dollars each. How much money will she have left?

Equation: _____________________

____

Remembering

Write an equation. Then solve the problem.   *Show your work.*

1. The Parkers' lawn is 10 yards long by 9 yards wide. They want to build a patio that is 4 yards by 5 yards. How many square yards of lawn will the Parkers have left when the patio is done?

   Equation: ___________________________________

   ____

2. Sarah sleeps 10 hours each night. Julio sleeps only 8 hours each night. How much more sleep does Sarah get in a week than Julio?

   Equation: ___________________________________

   ____

Complete the Scrambled Multiplication Table below.

×										
	49	7	70	14	28		56	21	35	
	70	10		20	40	60	80		50	90
		1	10	2	4	6	8	3		9
		6	60		24	36	48	18	30	54
	14	2	20	4		12	16	6	10	18
	56		80	16	32	48		24	40	72
	21	3	30		12	18	24	9		27
	28		40	8	16	24	32		20	36
	63	9		18		54		27	45	81
		5	50	10	20	30	40	15	25	

    Equations with Parentheses

Name ___________________________ **Date** ___________________________

Homework

Solve each problem. *Show your work.*

1. Michael has 21 T-shirts. One third of them are blue. How many of Michael's T-shirts are blue?

   ____

2. A gift-wrapping department has 4 colors of ribbon, 2 kinds of bows, and 7 kinds of wrapping paper. How many different gift-wrap styles are possible?

   ____

3. Anne-Marie has saved 9 dollars for a new coat. That is $\frac{1}{6}$ as much money as she needs. How much does the coat cost?

   ____

4. Last year it rained on 63 days in Mudville. There were 7 times as many days of rain in Mudville as in Desert Hills. How many days did it rain in Desert Hills last year?

   ____

5. Mrs. Ricardo makes toy cars to sell at craft fairs. She has 8 colors of paint, 5 body styles, and 2 kinds of wheels. How many different kinds of cars can she make?

   ____

6. At a country-music concert, 48 people played guitars. That number is 6 times as many as the number of people who played banjos. How many people at the concert played banjos?

   ____

7. There are 8 apples left on the table. There are $\frac{1}{4}$ as many apples as bananas left on the table. How many bananas are there?

   ____

Name   **Date**

Remembering

Use the pictograph and key to solve.

Bob, Reza, and Yoshi run laps around the track every day after school. This pictograph shows how many laps they ran last week.

Bob	👟 👟 👟 👟 👟 👟
Reza	👟 👟 👟 👟 👟 👟 👟 👟
Yoshi	👟 👟 👟 👟 👟

Key: 👟 = 8 laps

1. How many laps did Reza run last week? _______________________

2. How many more laps did Bob run than Yoshi? _______________________

3. How many more or fewer laps did Bob and Yoshi together run than Reza?

   ____

4. Yoshi ran the same number of laps every day except Friday, when he ran 12 laps. How many laps did he run on Wednesday?

   ____

Complete the Scrambled Multiplication Table.

5.

×										
	18						21			
			30						90	
					20			2		
						56				28
				20				4		
		16				64			72	
				30			42			
			3							4
		18					63			
	30				50					

      Combinations and Comparisons

Homework

Solve each problem. Label your answer.

1. Rachel has 4 times as many markers as Polly has. Rachel has 36 markers. How many markers does Polly have?

2. Sean sold 63 balloons at the fair. That is 7 times as many as Oscar sold. How many balloons did Oscar sell?

3. Ramon scored 72 points in basketball games this year. His friend Paco scored $\frac{1}{8}$ as many points as Ramon. How many points did Paco score?

4. Chris has 6 different cookie cutters, 4 kinds of frosting, and 2 kinds of sprinkles. How many different kinds of cookies can she make?

5. Meg and Kurt are building a tree house. They have 3 kinds of roofing material, 4 colors of paint, and 2 doors to choose from. How many different ways could they build the tree house?

6. Mrs. Grant's garden is a square that is 5 yards on each side. Mrs. Diego's garden is a square that is 10 yards on each side. The area of Mrs. Diego's garden is how many times as large as the area of Mrs. Grant's garden?

Solve each Factor Puzzle.

7. 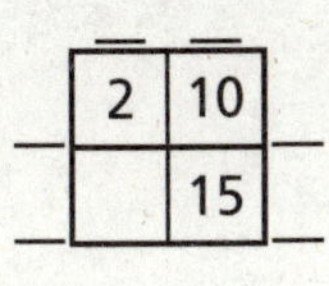

8. 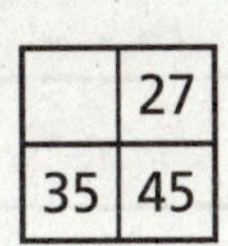

9. 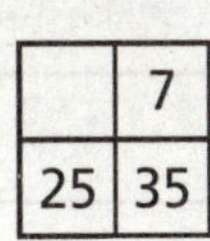

10. 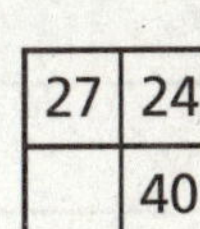

11. 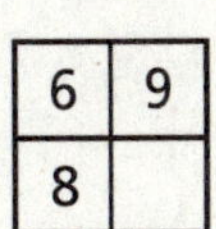

12. 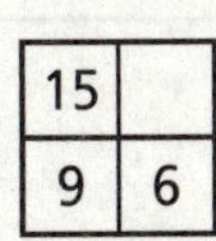

13.

14.

15. On a separate sheet of paper, write a Factor Puzzle for your classmates to solve. You may use a Multiplication Table.

Name ___________________________ **Date** ___________________________

Remembering

Complete.

1. Write the next two numbers: 9, 18, 27, _______, _______

2. If you multiply 51 × 51, will your answer be even or odd? _______ How do you know? ___________________________

3. If 52 × 38 = 1,976, then what is 1,976 ÷ 38? _______

4. What is b in this equation: 15 × 7 = 21 × b? _______

5. What is b in this equation: 5 × 6 = 5 × 4 + 5 × b? _______

6. If one person counts by 4s to 80 and another person counts by 8s to 80, will any of those numbers be the same? Explain which ones.

   ____

   ____

   ____

7. Which two of these answers cannot be right? How do you know?

   a. 18 × 17 = 305   **b.** 21 × 21 = 441   **c.** 32 × 48 = 1,535

   ____

   ____

   ____

   ____

Find the unknown number in each equation.

8. $8a = 48$

   $a =$ _______

9. $5b + 1 = 46$

   $b =$ _______

10. $3 \times (6 + 2) = d$

    $d =$ _______

11. $7e - 2 = 47$

    $e =$ _______

12. $\frac{1}{3}g = 8$

    $g =$ _______

13. $16 + h = 24$

    $h =$ _______

   Practice with Factors

Homework

Solve.   *Show your work.*

1. A fruit company makes two gift boxes of oranges—the Ruby Box and the Emerald Box. The Ruby Box has 8 rows and 6 columns of oranges. The Emerald Box has 7 rows and 7 columns of oranges. Which box has more oranges? How many more?

____

2. On his camping trip, Gus saw 18 hawks. He saw 6 times as many hawks as owls. How many owls did Gus see?

____

3. Melissa collected three kinds of autumn leaves when she was out walking today—elm, maple, and oak. She has 2 times as many maple leaves as elm leaves and 5 times as many oak leaves as elm leaves. Altogether, she has 32 leaves. How many of each kind does she have?

____

4. Everyone at Luke's party has 2 balloons except Ashley, because one of her balloons popped. There are 17 balloons at the party. How many people are at the party?

____

5. Patty bought 5 harmonicas for 3 dollars each and 4 whistles for 3 dollars each. How much money did Patty spend?

____

Find the unknown number in each equation. Write a 1 in front of an unknown that is alone if it will help you.

6. $c + 3c = 32$ ____

7. $6d - 3d + 2d = 35$ ____

8. $5a - a - 2a = 18$ ____

Remembering

Find the unknown number in each equation below.

1. $6h + 3h = 63$

$h =$ _______

2. $5(4 \times 2) = g$

$g =$ _______

3. $l = (2 \times 8) - (3 \times 2)$

$l =$ _______

4. $m + 3m = 28$

$m =$ _______

5. $56 \div r = 8$

$r =$ _______

6. $\frac{1}{8}b = 6$

$b =$ _______

7. $s = 9(7 - 2)$

$s =$ _______

8. $4d + d = 45$

$d =$ _______

9. $8w - 4w = 20$

$w =$ _______

Write *odd* or *even*.

10. The product of two even numbers is an _______ number.

11. The product of an odd number and an even number is an _______ number.

12. The product of two odd numbers is an _______ number.

Write an equation and use it to solve the problem.

13. A rectangle has an area of 48 sq cm and a length of 16 cm. What is the width of the rectangle?

____

14. A rectangle has a width of 10 inches and an area of 5 square inches. What is the length of the rectangle?

____

Solve. Explain your answer.

15. A stamp collector is arranging 100 stamps in rows with the same number of stamps in each row. How many different ways could she arrange the stamps if she would like more than 2 rows but fewer than 10 rows?

____

____

____

Multistep Problems

Homework

Use the Commutative Property to solve for *n* in these equations.

1. $45 \times 7 = 7 \times n$

$n =$ _______

2. $n \times 8 = 8 \times 29$

$n =$ _______

3. $36 \times n = 9 \times 36$

$n =$ _______

Use the Associative Property to solve each problem.

4. $(9 \times 3) \times 3 =$ _______________

5. $2 \times (5 \times 7) =$ _______________

6. $(8 \times 4) \times 2 =$ _______________

Use the Distributive Property to write each problem with only two factors. Then solve the problems.

7. $(7 \times 3) + (7 \times 5) =$ _______________

8. $(3 \times 9) + (4 \times 9) =$ _______________

9. $(8 \times 5) + (8 \times 4) =$ _______________

10. $(2 \times 6) + (8 \times 6) =$ _______________

Solve.

11. For Fall Festival, Mrs. Marco bought 6 bags of Golden Delicious apples. She handed out 43 apples and had 5 left over. How many apples were in each bag?

12. Juice boxes are sold in packs of 6. Tony brought 5 packs of juice boxes to a party, and Victor brought 4 packs. How many juice boxes are there at the party altogether?

13. Everyone in Mrs. Bowman's art class has 8 jars of paint except Jerome, who has 10. There are 74 jars of paint in the room. How many students are there in Mrs. Bowman's art class?

14. Lisa needs to make 2 times as many tuna as cheese sandwiches and 4 times as many ham as cheese sandwiches. If Lisa makes 56 sandwiches, how many of each of the 3 kinds will she make?

Name ___________   Date ___________

Remembering

Find the unknown number in each equation.

1. $4h + 5h = 63$

$h = $ _______

2. $4(2 \times 5) = g$

$g = $ _______

3. $4 \times (5 + 1) = i$

$i = $ _______

4. $l = (2 \times 6) - (4 \times 2)$

$l = $ _______

5. $m + 4m = 25$

$m = $ _______

6. $(48 \div 8) - 3 = p$

$p = $ _______

7. $72 \div r = 8$

$r = $ _______

8. $\frac{1}{8}b = 5$

$b = $ _______

9. $k = (3 \times 9) - (5 \times 0)$

$k = $ _______

10. $s = 8(9 - 2)$

$s = $ _______

11. $6d + d = 42$

$d = $ _______

12. $r = 17 + (6 \times 5)$

$r = $ _______

Complete each Factor Puzzle.

13.

	6
8	16

14.

	4
5	15

For each function table, write the rule in words and as an equation.
Then complete the table.

15.

Rule in Words						
Equation						
Number of people (p)	1	2		4		6	7
Number of feet (f)	2		6	8	10	12	

16.

Rule in Words						
Equation						
Number of eyes (e)	0		3	5	6		10
Number of legs (l)		6	9	15		24	30

     Properties of Multiplication

Homework

1. Connections

Jill has four of her five game scores:

8, 6, 6, 3

Her average score for the five games is 6 points. What is the fifth game score? Write an equation to help solve the problem.

____

____

____

2. Representation

Tyler is looking at a map. He wants to stop at three towns on Highway 57. Town A is 15 miles from Town B. Town A is 26 miles from Town C. Town B is between Towns A and C. How many miles are between Towns B and C? Draw a picture to support your answer.

____

3. Communication

The students are selling tickets to the School Fair. All tickets cost the same amount. Carly sold 3 tickets for a total of $9. Karen sold 6 tickets for a total of $18. Brendan sold 4 tickets for a total of $12. Use a function table to find the price per ticket and the total cost of 9 tickets. Show the rule and the equation you used to find the costs.

____

____

____

4. Reasoning and Proof

Lilly wrote the equation below to demonstrate the Commutative Property.

$(2 + 3) + (3 + 4) = (3 + 4) + (2 + 3)$

Does her equation demonstrate the Commutative Property? Explain why or why not.

____

____

____

Remembering

Find the unknown number in each equation.

1. $25 - (3 + 6) + (2 \times 4) = c$

$c =$ _______

2. $5a - 3a = 18$

$a =$ _______

3. $g = 7(10 - 3)$

$g =$ _______

4. $63 \div (26 - 19) = w$

$w =$ _______

5. $6 + y = 17$

$y =$ _______

6. $4 = \frac{1}{2}v$

$v =$ _______

7. $27 = 8k + k$

$k =$ _______

8. $9(4 + 5) = e$

$e =$ _______

9. $5q = 35$

$q =$ _______

10. $m = 11 + (3 \times 8) - (4 \times 6)$

$m =$ _______

11. $12r - 4r = 48$

$r =$ _______

12. $\frac{1}{6}h = 9$

$h =$ _______

Solve. Show your work.

13. You know that $8 \times 9 = 72$. How can you use this to find the product of 8×8? _______________________________

14. On Monday, Hugo read 4 pages. On Tuesday, he read three times as many pages as on Monday. On Wednesday, he read twice as many pages as on Monday. How many pages did Hugo read in all during the three days?

____

15. Carmen bought 3 boxes of pencils. Each box has the same number of pencils. She used 5 pencils and had 7 pencils left over. How many pencils were in each box?

____

16. Belle bought packages of beads for her project. Ben bought twice as many packages as Belle. Micalla bought three times as many packages as Belle. Altogether, they bought 24 packages of beads. How many packages did each person buy?

____

17. Kari is 10 years old. Her sister is half her age. Explain why $10 \times \frac{1}{2}$ can be used to find her sister's age.

____

____

Homework

1. How many decimeters make 1 meter? _____________________

2. How many square decimeters make 1 square meter? _____________________

3. How many centimeters make 1 meter? _____________________

4. How many square centimeters make 1 square meter? _____________________

5. How many millimeters make 1 meter? _____________________

6. How many square millimeters make 1 square meter? _____________________

Find the area of each rectangle. Show your work.

7.
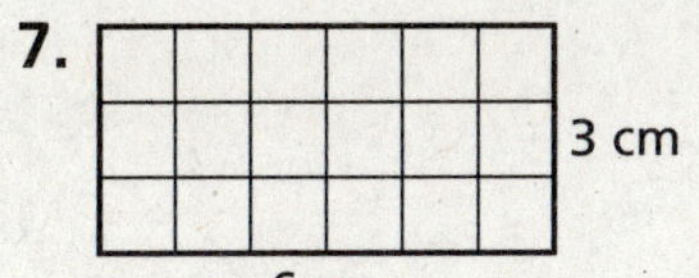

8.
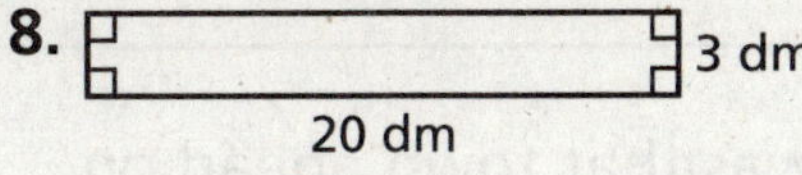

9.
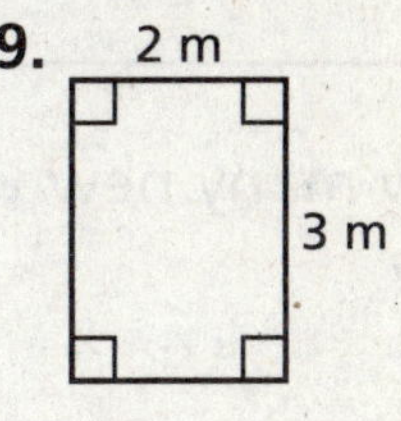

_____________________   _____________________   _____________________

_____________________   _____________________   _____________________

10. Jason is tiling a patio. The tiles are each 1 square decimeter.
The patio is 6 meters long and 4 meters wide. How many
tiles will Jason need?

____

What metric unit would you use to find each?

11. the area of a gymnasium _______   12. the length of a pencil _______

13. the area of a door _______   14. the length of an eyelash _______

15. the area of a book cover _______   16. the area of a driveway _______

Remembering

Marville and Geotown had a new voter registration
contest. The pictograph shows the results by day.

Marville on Friday	
Geotown on Friday	
Marville on Saturday	
Geotown on Saturday	
Marville on Sunday	
Geotown on Sunday	

Key: ▤ = 8 new voters

Use the pictograph and key to solve.

1. Which town was in the lead on Friday?

____

2. By how many new voters was that town ahead on
Friday?

____

3. How many more new voters were registered on Sunday
in Marville than in Geotown?

____

Solve the problems below. Make a drawing if it helps.   *Show your work.*

4. Ramon planted 3 rows of seeds. He put 8 seeds in each
row. Each row of seeds was 42 inches long. How far
apart did Ramon plant the seeds?

____

5. Bunches of 6 roses were selling for $8. Anita paid $40
for roses. How many roses did she buy?

____

6. Ms. Goldfarb has 12 turquoise beads and 3 times as
many amber beads. She is making 8 pins with the same
number of beads on each pin. How many beads will
be on a pin?

____

Homework

Find the perimeter and area of each rectangle.

1.

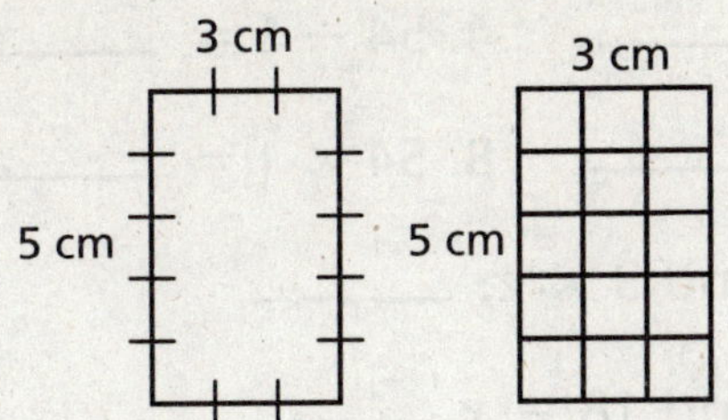

P = __________________

A = __________________

2.

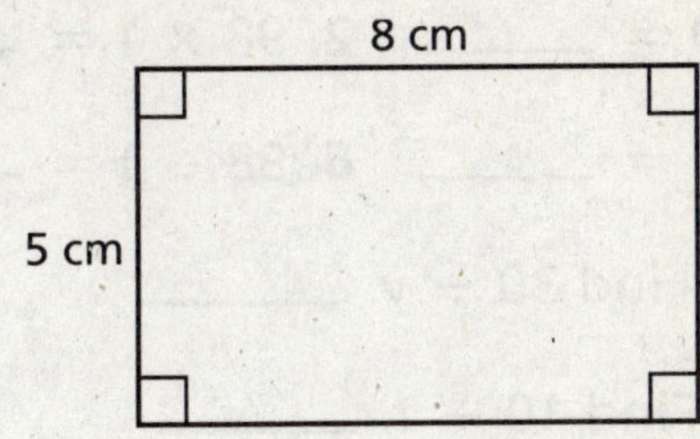

P = __________________

A = __________________

3.

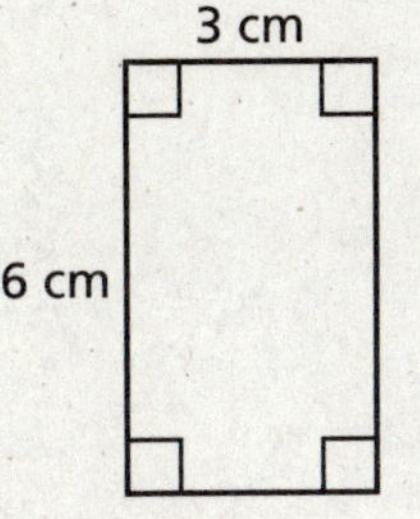

P = __________________

A = __________________

4.

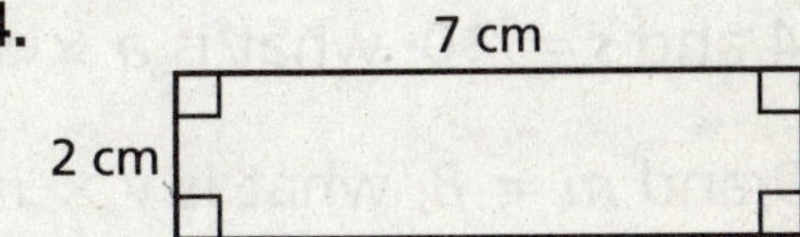

P = __________________

A = __________________

5.

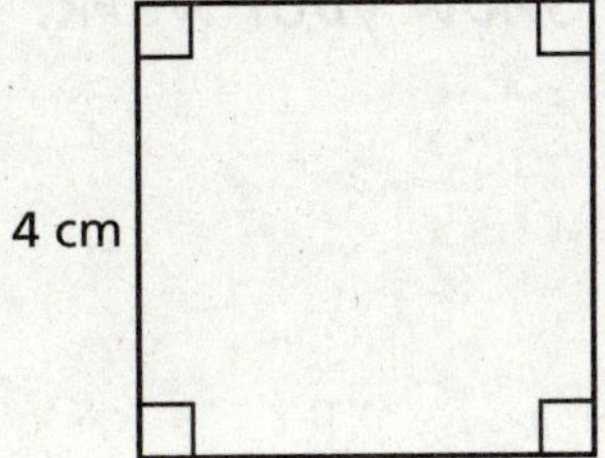

P = __________________

A = __________________

Solve the word problem.

6. Kaya is wallpapering one wall of her room. The wall is 10 feet long and 8 feet tall. How many square feet of wallpaper will Kaya need? ______________________________________

7. Kaya's room is 12 feet long and 10 feet wide. She wants to put a border at the top of the walls. How many feet of border does she need? ______________________________________

Remembering

Solve.

1. $18 \times 0 = $ _____   2. $98 \times 1 = $ _____   3. $0 \div 85 = $ _____   4. $54 \div 1 = $ _____

5. $0 \div 22 = $ _____   6. $98 \div 1 = $ _____   7. $0 \times 14 = $ _____   8. $54 \times 1 = $ _____

9. $y = 5$. Find $30 \div y$. _____   10. $z = 7$. Find $3 \times z$. _____

11. $t = 2$. Find $10 \div t$. _____   12. $x = 6$. Find $18 \div x$. _____

13. $s = 11$. Find $5 \times s$. _____   14. $u = 8$. Find $6 \times u$. _____

15. If $h = 12$ and $t = 36$, what is $t \div h$? _____

16. If $a = 4$ and $s = 10$, what is $a \times s$? _____

17. If $v = 9$ and $m = 8$, what is $v \times m$? _____

18. If $u = 77$ and $d = 7$, what is $u \div d$? _____

19. If $s = 20$ and $t = 4$, what is $s \div t$? _____

20. If $m = 12$ and $p = 5$, what is $m \times p$? _____

Solve the problems below.

Show your work.

21. Simon bought 4 packages of holiday greeting cards. Each package was $6. How much did he spend?

____

22. Simon's packages contained 36 cards altogether. How many cards were in each package?

____

23. Each package contained 3 different designs of cards. How many cards of each design did Simon buy?

____

____

Remember to use your Target and Division Cards to practice.

    Perimeter and Area of Rectangles

Homework

1. Look at the parallelograms. Which two parallelograms have the same area? Show your work.

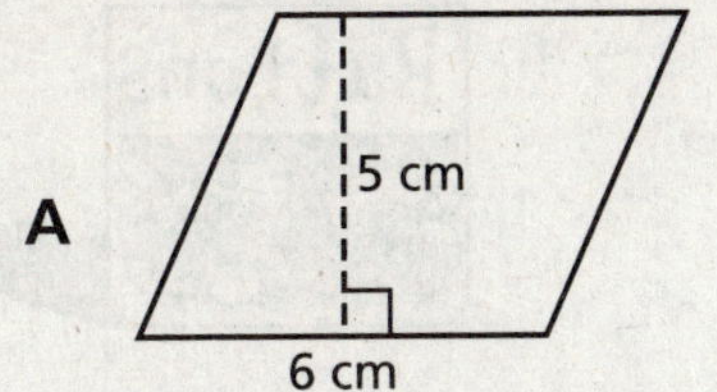

B

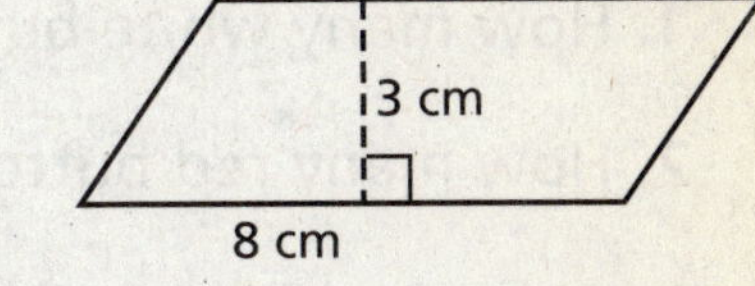

2. Look at the right triangles. Which two triangles have the same area? Show your work.

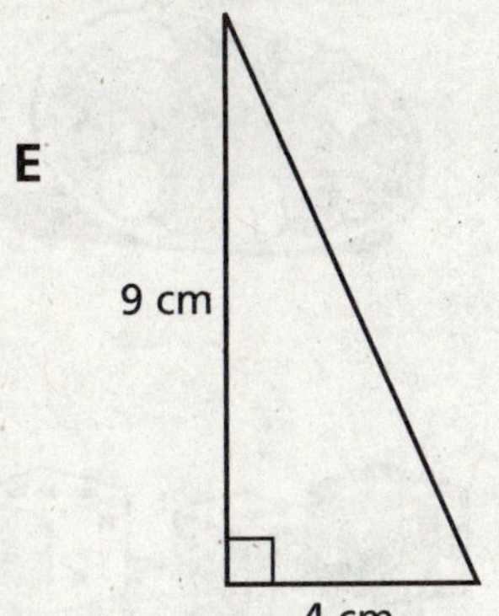

F

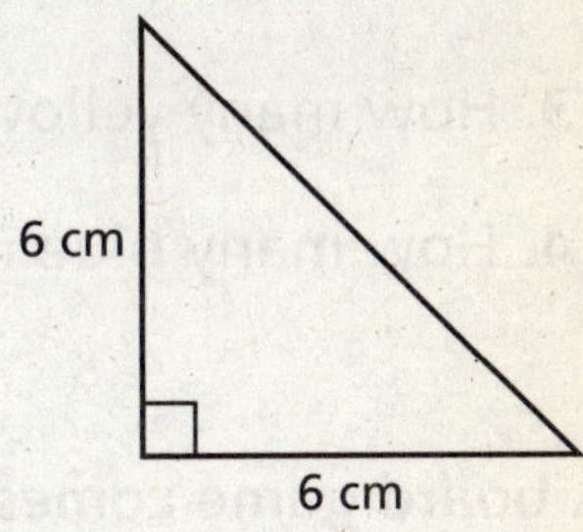

3. For each right triangle, draw the rectangle made by drawing sides opposite the two shorter sides in the triangle. Find the area of each rectangle.

4. How does the area of each rectangle relate to the area of either right triangle inside it?

____

Remembering

There are 36 buttons in a jar. There are 3 times as many red buttons as white buttons.

1. How many white buttons are there? _______

2. How many red buttons are there? _______

Hint: Let w = the number of white buttons
       and $3w$ = the number of red buttons.

There are 40 yellow and blue marbles in a bag. There are 4 times as many blue marbles as yellow marbles.

3. How many yellow marbles are there? _______

4. How many blue marbles are there? _______

A board game comes with 9 white and green number cubes. There are twice as many white cubes as green cubes.

5. How many green number cubes are there? _______

6. How many white number cubes are there? _______

There are 30 bows in a bag. There are 5 times as many small bows as large bows.

7. How many large bows are there? _______

8. How many small bows are there? _______

There are 20 red and blue pens in a box. There are 3 times as many blue pens as red pens.

9. How many red pens are there? _______

10. How many blue pens are there? _______

Homework

Name ___________ **Date** ___________

Find the area of each triangle.

1.
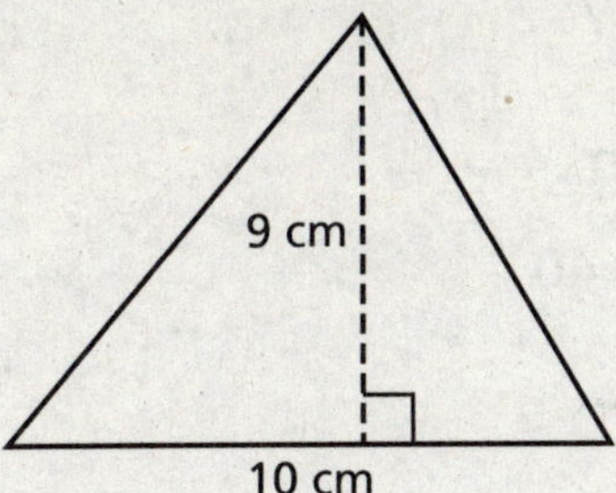

____

2.
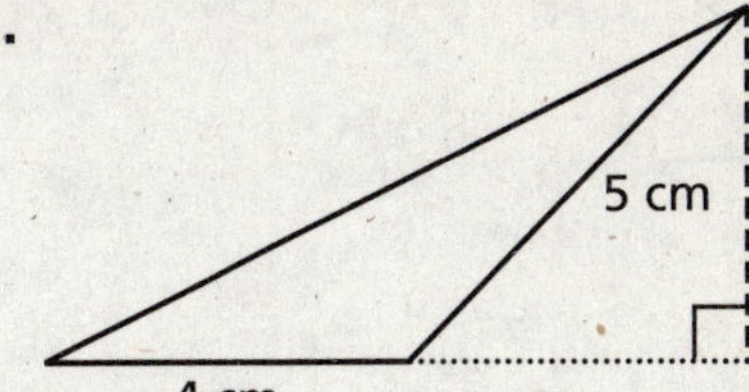

____

3.
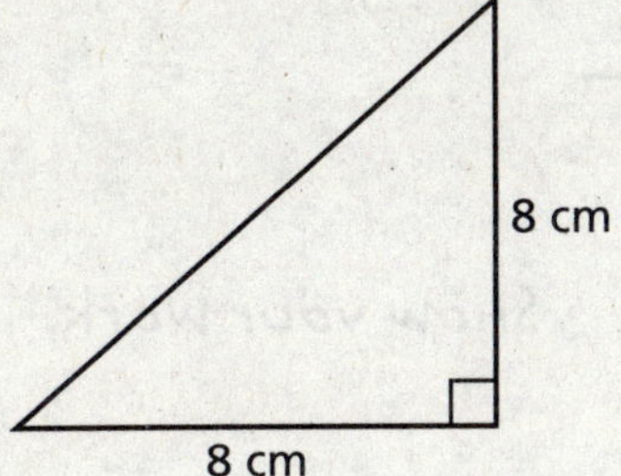

____

4.
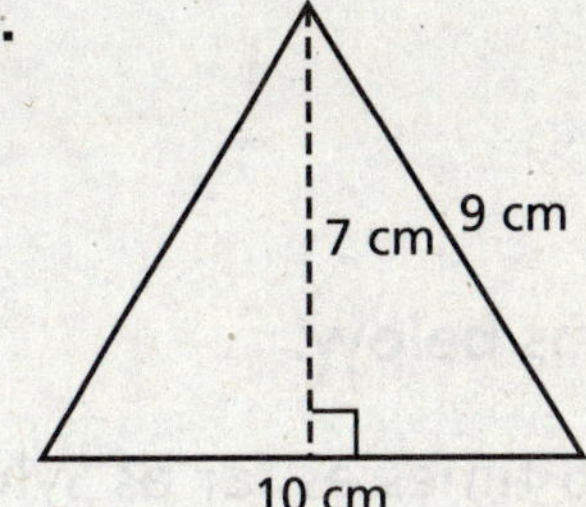

____

5.
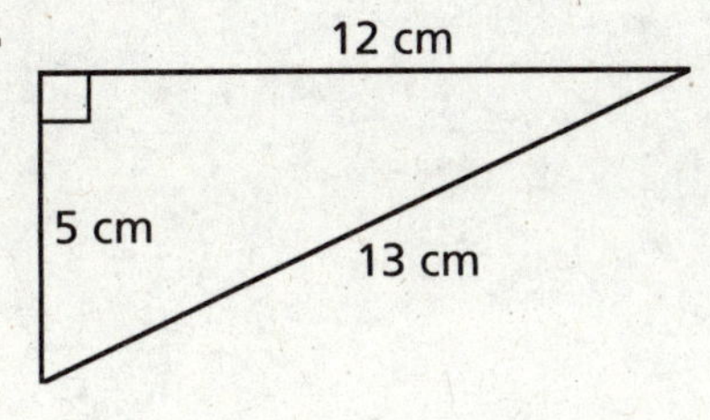

____

6.
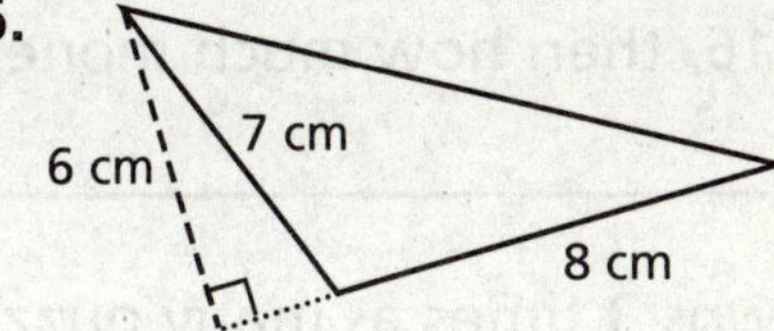

____

The Area of Any Triangle **41**

Name **Date**

Remembering

Find the unknown number.

1. $k \div 7 = 8$

   $k =$ _______

2. $63 \div s = 7$

   $s =$ _______

3. $21 = 3d$

   $d =$ _______

4. $32 + p = 40$

   $p =$ _______

5. $z = (8 \times 8) + (2 \times 5)$

   $z =$ _______

6. $4c + 2 = 18$

   $c =$ _______

7. $t = 7 \times (6 + 3)$

   $t =$ _______

8. $12 - (10 - 3) = w$

   $w =$ _______

Solve the problems below.

Show your work.

9. Julie walked 6 times as far as Sylvia. If Sylvia walked 5 km, then how far did Julie walk?

   ____

10. Andrew spent half as much money as Justin. If Justin spent $16, then how much money did Andrew spend?

   ____

11. Brian owns 3 times as many puzzles as Jenna. If Jenna has 4 puzzles, then how many puzzles does Brian own?

   ____

12. Emilio has 3 times as many coins as Anna. If Emilio has 27 coins, then how many coins does Anna have?

   ____

The Area of Any Triangle

Homework

Name ___________________________ **Date** ___________________________

Find the perimeter and area.

1. 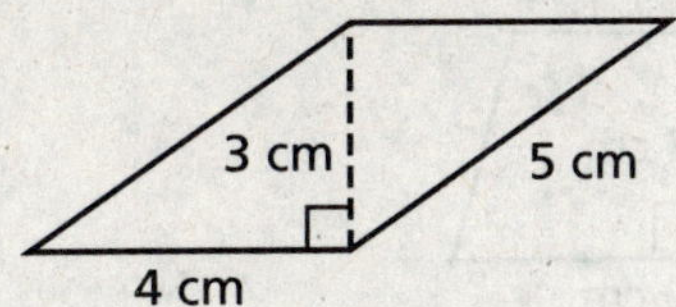

P = ___________

A = ___________

2. 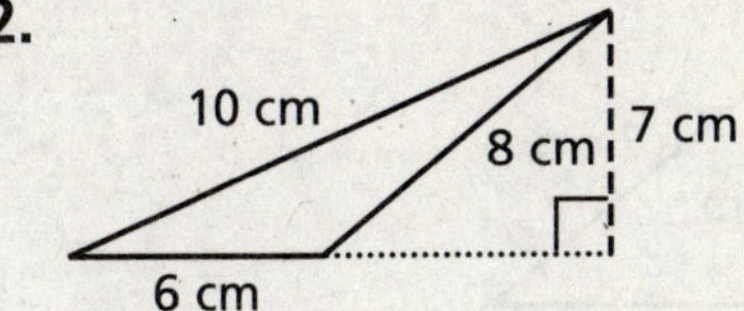

P = ___________

A = ___________

3. 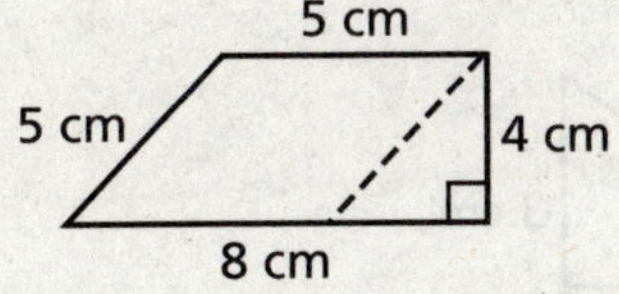

P = ___________

A = ___________

4. 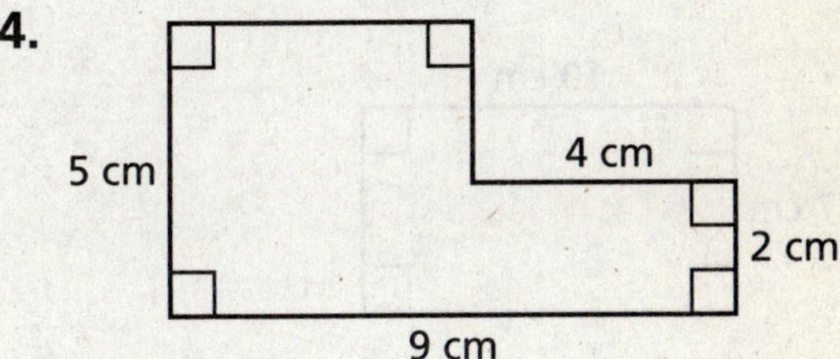

P = ___________

A = ___________

5. 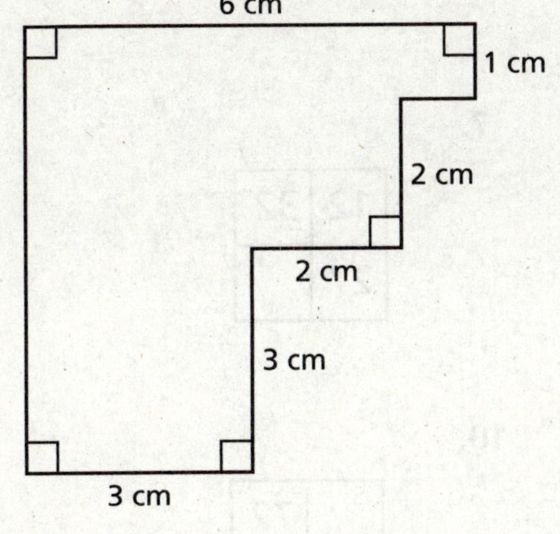

P = ___________

A = ___________

6. 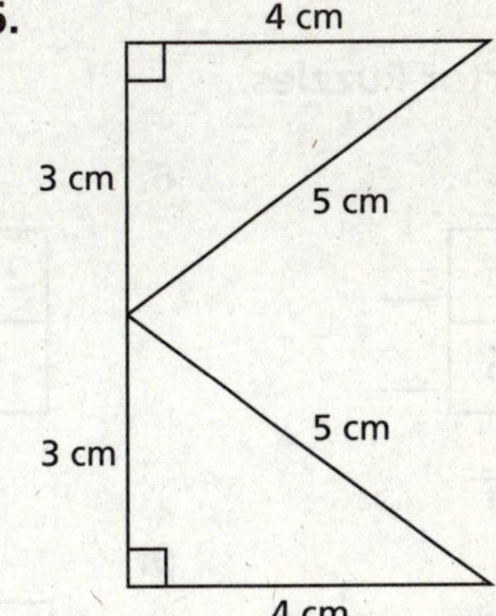

P = ___________

A = ___________

  Consolidate Perimeter and Area **43**

Remembering

Find the perimeter and area.

1.
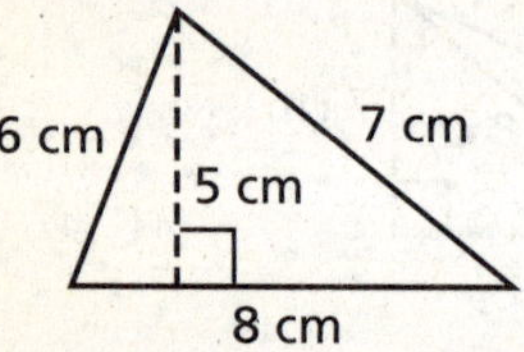

P = _____________

A = _____________

2.
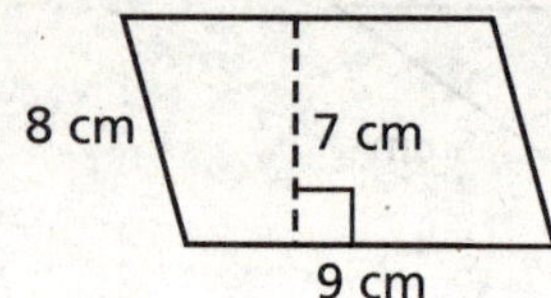

P = _____________

A = _____________

3.
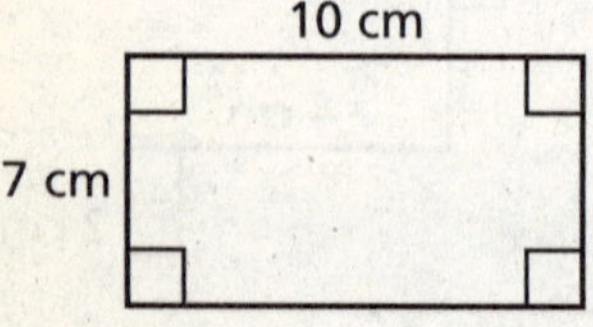

P = _____________

A = _____________

4.
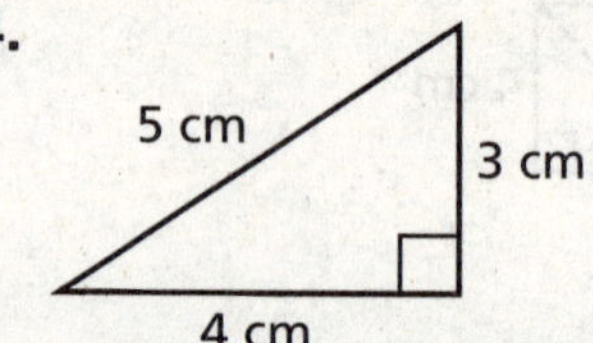

P = _____________

A = _____________

Solve the Factor Puzzles.

5.
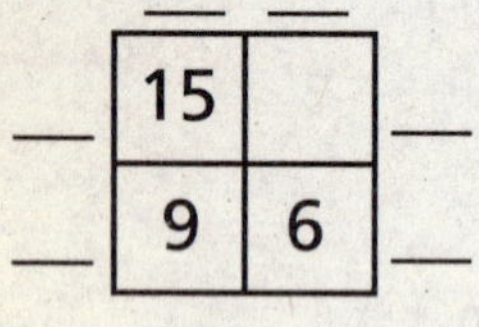

6.

25	50
	30

7.

12	32
27	

8.

49	28
63	

9.

56	
49	63

10.

	72
28	32

Consolidate Perimeter and Area

Homework

Complete.

1. 36 in. = _______ ft   2. 12 ft = _______ yd   3. 36 in. = _______ yd

4. _______ in. = 4 ft   5. _______ ft = 2 yd   6. _______ in. = 3 yd

Find the perimeter and area of each figure in feet.

7.
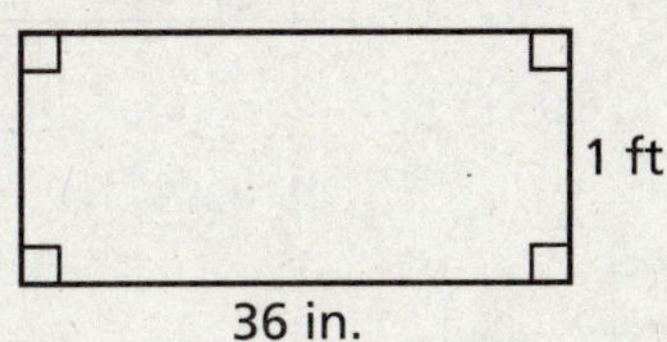

$P =$ _____________

$A =$ _____________

8.
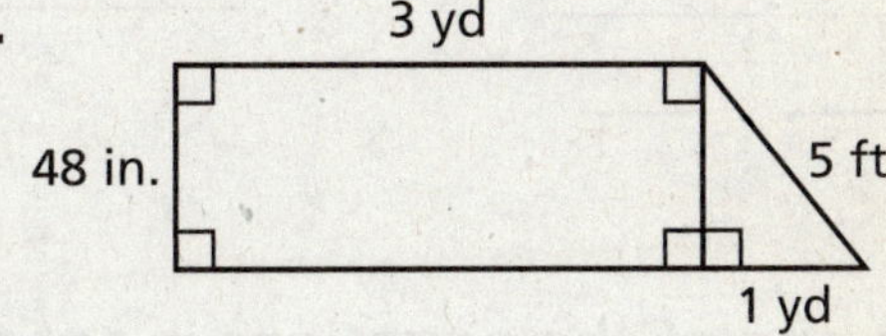

$P =$ _____________

$A =$ _____________

Find the perimeter and area of each figure in yards.

9.
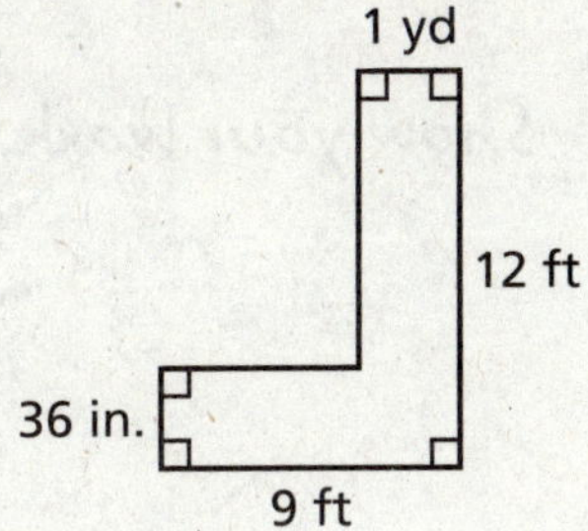

$P =$ _____________

$A =$ _____________

10.
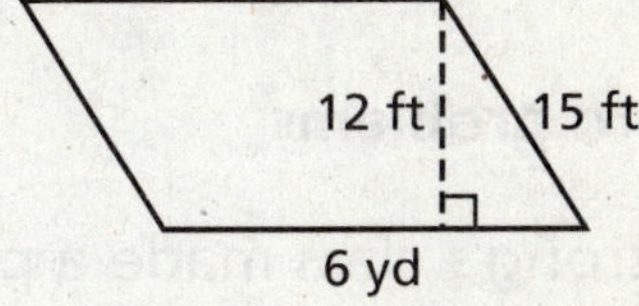

$P =$ _____________

$A =$ _____________

Remembering

Solve the Factor Puzzles.

1. 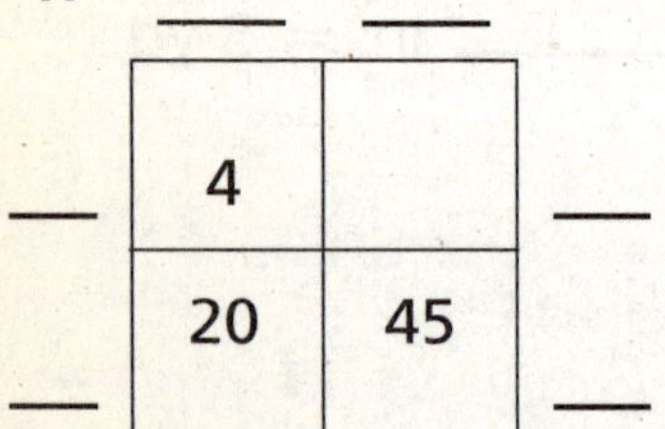

2.

	7
24	12

3.

	9
48	54

4.

16	18
	81

Which one of the equations is not true? _________________________
Explain your answer.

5. $9 \times 3 = 3 \times 9$ **6.** $9 + 3 = 3 + 9$ **7.** $9 \div 3 = 3 \div 9$

____

____

Solve the word problems.   *Show your work.*

8. Mrs. Armstrong's class made a paper chain that is 15 feet long. They want to put it around the bulletin board. The bulletin board is 4 feet long and 3 feet wide. Is the chain long enough to go all the way around? How do you know?

____

____

____

9. The Sanchez family is building a sandbox 6 feet long and 4 feet wide. How many square feet will the sandbox cover?

____

Homework

The following shows how place value and money are related.

ones	.	tenths	hundredths	thousandths
($1.00)		(dimes)	(pennies)	(tenths of a penny)

Write each fraction as a decimal and then say it.

1. $\frac{349}{1,000}$ _______

2. $\frac{6}{10}$ _______

3. $\frac{58}{100}$ _______

4. $\frac{27}{1,000}$ _______

5. $\frac{2}{10}$ _______

6. $\frac{9}{100}$ _______

7. $\frac{6}{1,000}$ _______

8. $\frac{71}{100}$ _______

9. $\frac{90}{100}$ _______

10. $\frac{843}{1,000}$ _______

11. $\frac{5}{10}$ _______

12. $\frac{4}{100}$ _______

13. $\frac{1}{1,000}$ _______

14. $\frac{45}{100}$ _______

15. $\frac{896}{1,000}$ _______

16. $\frac{58}{1,000}$ _______

Solve.

17. A large building has 1,000 windows, and 5 of the windows need to be replaced. What decimal represents the number of windows that need to be replaced?

____

18. At a reception, 23 of 100 pieces of wedding cake have been eaten. What decimal number represents the number of pieces of cake that have been eaten?

____

19. Jody made 10 party invitations. Yesterday she mailed 4 of them. What decimal represents the number of invitations that have been mailed?

____

20. There are 1,000 vehicles in a stadium parking lot; 422 of the vehicles are trucks. What decimal represents the number of vehicles that are trucks?

____

Remembering

Solve for each unknown.

1. $9 \times w = 63$

$w =$ _______

2. $42 \div 7 = c$

$c =$ _______

3. $q \times 8 = 40$

$q =$ _______

4. $k \div 6 = 9$

$k =$ _______

5. $7d = 56$

$d =$ _______

6. $28 \div 4 = x$

$x =$ _______

7. $6 \cdot 8 = h$

$h =$ _______

8. $36 \div z = 9$

$z =$ _______

9. $8 \cdot g = 72$

$g =$ _______

In each table, write a multiplication rule. Include two variables in each rule you write. Then complete the table.

10.

Rule:					
Number of packages (*p*)	3	5	8		11
Number of erasers (*e*)	27		72	90	

11.

Rule:					
Number of rows (*r*)	2	4	6		
Number of seats (*s*)	16	32		64	88

Solve.

12. Lyle found the area of the figure on the right to be 34 in.² and the perimeter to be 40 in. Is he correct? If not, explain how to find each correct answer.

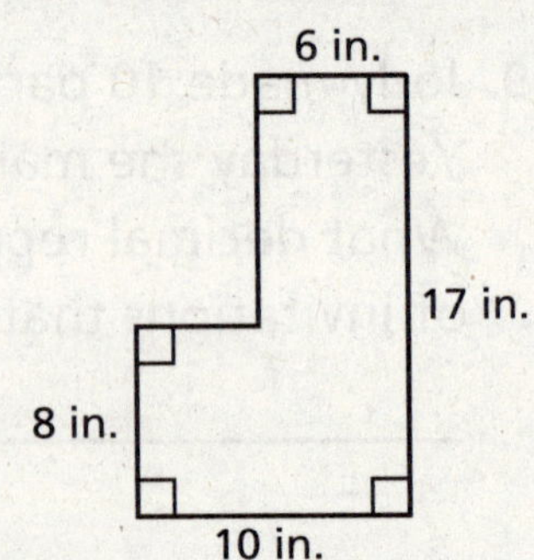

____

____

13. Julio earned $\frac{1}{4}$ the number of points as Paulos. If Julio earned 8 points, how many points did Paulos earn?

____

　　Decimals as Equal Divisions

Homework

Name ___________________ **Date** ___________________

Write each amount as a decimal number.

1. 9 tenths _______

2. 52 thousandths _______

3. 8 hundredths _______

4. 3 cents _______

5. $\frac{65}{100}$ _______

6. $\frac{548}{1,000}$ _______

7. $\frac{12}{1,000}$ _______

8. $\frac{7}{100}$ _______

9. 4 thousandths _______

Circle the value that is *not* equivalent to the other values.

10. 0.47   0.470   0.407   0.4700

11. 0.5   0.50 $\frac{5}{10}$ 0.05

12. 0.801   0.810   0.81   0.8100

13. 0.700   0.70   0.07   0.7

14. 0.39   0.390 $\frac{39}{100}$ $\frac{39}{1,000}$

15. 0.04   0.40   0.040   0.0400

Compare. Write > (greater than) or < (less than).

16. 0.36 ◯ 0.8

17. 0.405 ◯ 0.62

18. 0.91 ◯ 0.95

19. 0.45 ◯ 0.4

20. 0.836 ◯ 0.83

21. 0.299 ◯ 0.3

22. 0.621 ◯ 0.612

23. 0.7 ◯ 0.07

24. 0.504 ◯ 0.54

A store had the same amount of five fabrics. The chart shows the how much of each fabric is left. Use the data to answer each question.

Red fabric	0.510 yd
Blue fabric	0.492 yd
Yellow fabric	0.6 yd
White fabric	0.51 yd
Black fabric	0.48 yd

25. The store sold the most of which fabric? Explain.

____

26. The store sold the least of which fabric? Explain.

____

27. The same amount of which fabrics is left? Explain.

____

Name   **Date**

Remembering

Solve for each unknown.

1. $h \times 7 = 49$

    $h =$ _______

2. $s \div 8 = 7$

    $s =$ _______

3. $8 \times b = 32$

    $b =$ _______

4. $48 \div 6 = x$

    $x =$ _______

5. $10 \cdot a = 0$

    $a =$ _______

6. $54 \div 9 = y$

    $y =$ _______

7. $5 \cdot 4 = d$

    $d =$ _______

8. $63 \div n = 9$

    $n =$ _______

9. $6 \cdot t = 36$

    $t =$ _______

10. $72 \div r = 9$

    $r =$ _______

11. $5 \times 9 = v$

    $v =$ _______

12. $\frac{27}{3} = m$

    $m =$ _______

Solve the Factor Puzzles.

13. 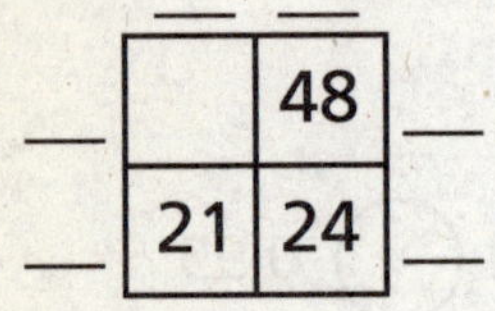

	48
21	24

14.

21	
63	54

15.

21	63
	36

Solve.

16. Franco is ordering lunch with a drink, sandwich, and a salad. He has a choice of 3 drinks, 2 sandwiches, and 4 salads. How many possible lunches are there?

____

17. Tamara has 4 times as many pages to read for her book report as Maria. Tamara has 20 pages left to read. How many pages does Maria have left to read?

____

18. Dae Youn wants to place new carpet in his room. The floor in his room has a width of 6 feet and a length of 10 feet. How much carpet does he need?

____

      Equate and Compare

Homework

Write a decimal number for each word name.

1. nine thousand, six hundred five and nine tenths

2. two hundred ten thousand, fifty and nineteen hundredths

3. three tenths

4. seven thousandths

5. eight hundredths

Write each amount as a decimal number.

6. $\frac{602}{1,000}$ _______

7. $\frac{21}{100}$ _______

8. $4\frac{9}{10}$ _______

9. $14\frac{27}{100}$ _______

10. $35\frac{712}{1,000}$ _______

11. $9\frac{5}{100}$ _______

12. $24\frac{13}{1,000}$ _______

13. $3\frac{68}{100}$ _______

14. $2\frac{1}{1,000}$ _______

15. $63\frac{7}{10}$ _______

16. $\frac{84}{1,000}$ _______

17. $29\frac{4}{1,000}$ _______

18. $8\frac{17}{1,000}$ _______

19. $\frac{6}{100}$ _______

20. $5\frac{106}{1,000}$ _______

21. $37\frac{3}{100}$ _______

Circle the value that is not equivalent to the other values.

22. 2.6   2.60   2.06   2.600

23. 4.07   4.070   4.70   4.0700

24. 65.800   65.8   65.08   65.80

25. 37.6   37.060   37.0600   37.06

Compare. Write > (greater than) or < (less than).

26. 14.08 ◯ 14.80

27. 789.152 ◯ 789.15

28. 3.071 ◯ 3.007

Order the decimal numbers from least to greatest.

29. 943.18, 94.18, 943.179, 94.183,

____

        Thousands to Thousandths **51**

Remembering

1. $6 \times a = 24$

$a =$ _______

2. $28 \div 7 = x$

$x =$ _______

3. $j \times 7 = 42$

$j =$ _______

4. $y \times 9 = 54$

$y =$ _______

5. $k \cdot 9 = 81$

$k =$ _______

6. $56 \div 8 = s$

$s =$ _______

7. $8 \cdot 5 = z$

$z =$ _______

8. $63 \div u = 9$

$u =$ _______

9. $6 \cdot n = 48$

$n =$ _______

Describe the angles that appear to be formed by the intersection of the lines as acute, obtuse or right.

10.

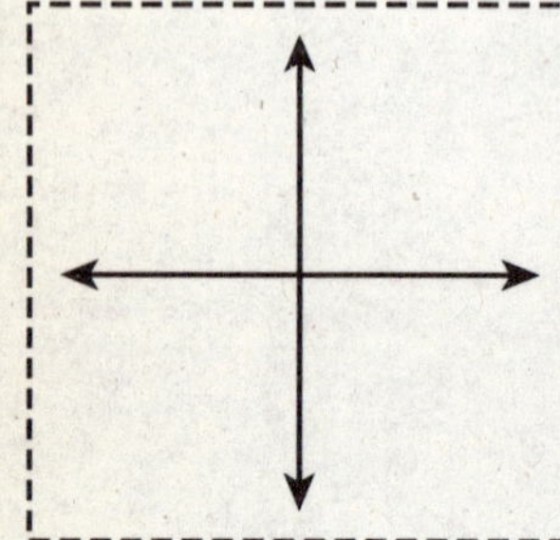

____

11.

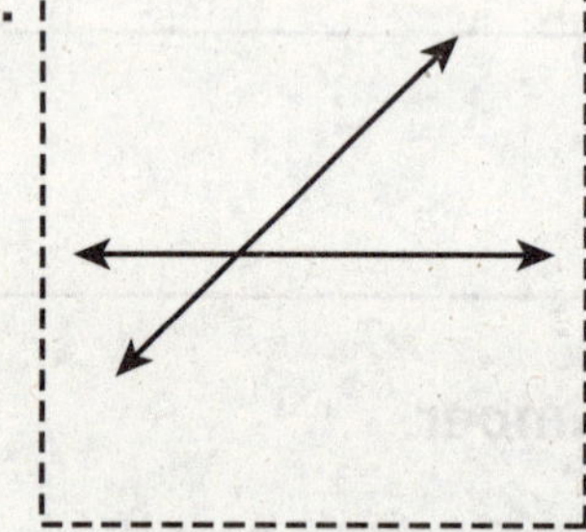

____

12. Erika drew a triangle having a base of 6 inches and a height of 8 inches. Trevor drew a square having a side measure of 5 inches. Rena drew a parallelogram having a base of 12 inches and a height of 2 inches.

Of the figures that were drawn, which has the greatest area? On the lines below, explain your answer.

Show your work.

> area of a parallelogram = base $\times$ height
>
> area of a square = side $\times$ side
>
> area of a triangle = $\dfrac{\text{base} \times \text{height}}{2}$

____

____

____

Homework

The chart at the right shows the average speed of four horses during a race. Use the data to answer each question.

Fast Jack	47.510 mph
Gold Dust	47.492 mph
Fire Brand	47.6 mph
Relentless	47.51 mph

1. Which horse had the greatest speed?

____

2. Which horse had the slowest speed?

____

3. Which horses had identical speeds?

____

Copy each exercise. Then add or subtract.

4. $0.9 + 0.06 =$ _______

5. $0.47 + 0.258 =$ _______

6. $0.56 + 0.913 =$ _______

7. $1.4 - 0.9 =$ _______

8. $5 - 1.5 =$ _______

9. $3.7 - 2.49 =$ _______

10. $0.008 + 0.6 =$ _______

11. $0.482 + 0.309 =$ _______

12. $19 + 1.044 =$ _______

13. $3 - 0.005 =$ _______

14. $0.409 - 0.20 =$ _______

15. $6.07 - 4 =$ _______

Remembering

Solve for each unknown.

1. $a \div 4 = 10$

$a = \underline{\hspace{2cm}}$

2. $3 \cdot c = 27$

$c = \underline{\hspace{2cm}}$

3. $24 \div d = 6$

$d = \underline{\hspace{2cm}}$

4. $e \times 9 = 36$

$e = \underline{\hspace{2cm}}$

5. $64 \div 8 = j$

$j = \underline{\hspace{2cm}}$

6. $8b = 16$

$b = \underline{\hspace{2cm}}$

7. $g = 5 \times 7$

$g = \underline{\hspace{2cm}}$

8. $7 = h \div 3$

$h = \underline{\hspace{2cm}}$

9. $30 = 6 \cdot r$

$r = \underline{\hspace{2cm}}$

10. $(16 - 7) \times 2 = m$

$m = \underline{\hspace{2cm}}$

11. $p = 16 - (7 \times 2)$

$p = \underline{\hspace{2cm}}$

12. $(2 \times 3) - (1 \times 5) = v$

$v = \underline{\hspace{2cm}}$

13. $2 \times (3 - 1) \times 5 = s$

$s = \underline{\hspace{2cm}}$

14. $w = (24 \div 3) + 9$

$w = \underline{\hspace{2cm}}$

15. $5 + 7 + (6 \div 3) = q$

$q = \underline{\hspace{2cm}}$

Solve.

16. Yoshi is making cards. He can choose from 4 colors of markers and 5 colors of paper. How many different ways can he create a card?

17. On the front of each card, Yoshi centers 3 rows with 6 stickers in each row. How many stickers does he use on the front of each card?

18. To make cards, Yoshi bought new markers. Each package he bought had 8 markers. He used 7 markers and had 25 markers left. How many package of markers did he buy?

19. Yoshi figured out that it costs him $2 for the supplies to make one card. So, he decided to sell each card for $5. If he sells 6 cards, how much does Yoshi earn in profit?

Name   **Date**

Homework

Compare. Write > (greater than) or < (less than).

1. 0.15 ◯ 0.9   **2.** 0.52 ◯ 0.307   **3.** 0.48 ◯ 0.6

4. 0.283 ◯ 0.238   **5.** 0.75 ◯ 1.4   **6.** 0.5 ◯ 0.05

7. 2 ◯ 0.2   **8.** 3.088 ◯ 3.1   **9.** 7.40 ◯ 4.7

Write each whole number.

10. 80 thousand = ______________   **11.** nine million = ______________

12. seven billion = ______________   **13.** 42 million, 120 = ______________

Copy each exercise. Then add.

14. 0.7 + 0.05 = ______   **15.** 0.48 + 0.159 = ______   **16.** 0.25 + 0.618 = ______

Copy each exercise. Then subtract.

17. 10 − 0.35 = ______   **18.** 0.7 − 0.19 = ______   **19.** 3.6 − 2 = ______

Write these related pairs.

20. 1 million ______________   **21.** 1 millionth ______________

22. 6 billion ______________   **23.** 6 billionth ______________

24. Write 2 ways in which whole numbers and decimal numbers are different.

____

____

____

Remembering

Solve for each unknown.

1. $s \times 4 = 16$

$s =$ _______

2. $d \div 2 = 10$

$d =$ _______

3. $7 \times e = 49$

$e =$ _______

4. $72 \div 9 = x$

$x =$ _______

5. $6 \cdot c = 42$

$c =$ _______

6. $54 \div 9 = r$

$r =$ _______

7. $8 \cdot 6 = v$

$v =$ _______

8. $32 \div g = 8$

$g =$ _______

9. $7 \cdot t = 63$

$t =$ _______

Write acute, right, or obtuse for each triangle.

10. 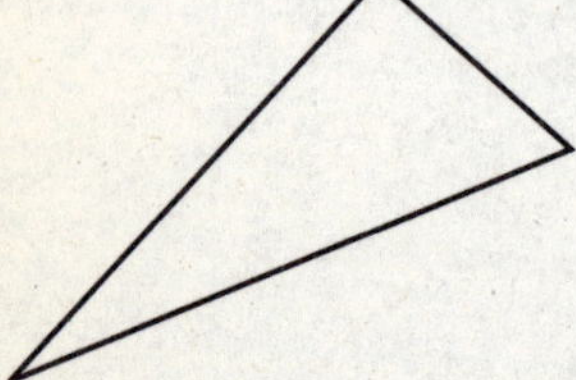

____

11. 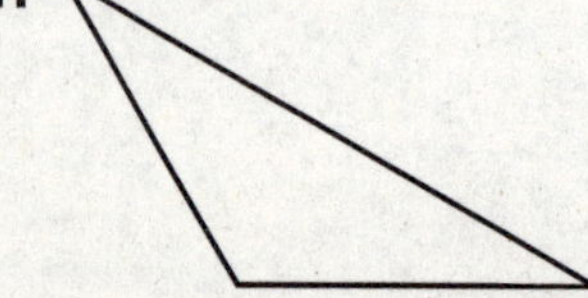

____

12. 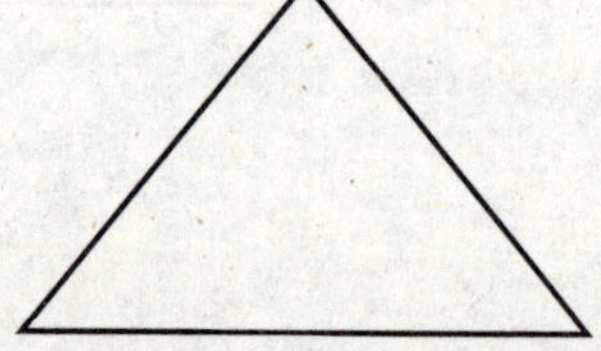

____

In each table, write a multiplication rule in words and as an equation with two variables. Then complete the table.

13.

Rule in words:					
Equation					
Hours (h)	1	2	3		6
Distance in miles (m)	10	20		50	60

14.

Rule in words:					
Equation					
Distance in feet (f)		1	4	2	5
Seconds (s)	0	2		4	10

    Billions to Billionths

Name _________________________ **Date** _________________________

Homework

Write the word name for each decimal number.

1. 0.06 ____

2. 24.7 ____

3. 1.308 ____

Follow the directions to change the number in the box.

$$\boxed{764,259.03}$$

4. Increase the number by 100,000. ____________

5. Decrease the number by 1 hundredth. ____________

6. Increase the number by 5 tenths. ____________

7. Write a number with 2 more in the ten thousands place. ____________

8. Rearrange the digits to make the greatest possible decimal number with two decimal places. ____________

Write each number.

9. five hundred thousand = ____________

10. 4 thousand and 6 tenths = ____________

11. 10 and 8 hundredths = ____________

12. 390 and 7 thousandths = ____________

Compare. Write > (greater than) or < (less than).

13. 657,894 ◯ 657,994

14. 120,705 ◯ 1,207,051

15. 3,246,000,800 ◯ 3,246,001,800

16. 4,900,754,001 ◯ 490,075,400

17. 7,504,180 ◯ 7,503,190

18. 27,546,709 ◯ 27,543,893

19. 91,257,306 ◯ 991,257,375

20. 638,697,345 ◯ 638,687,345

21. 1,753,682 ◯ 1,753,692

22. 8,004,752,390 ◯ 8,004,752,490

Remembering

Copy each exercise. Then add or subtract.

1. $23 + 1.75 =$ _______   **2.** $0.9 - 0.62 =$ _______   **3.** $0.41 + 0.007 =$ _______

4. $6.12 - 3.1 =$ _______   **5.** $5 + 2.01 =$ _______   **6.** $5 - 4.106 =$ _______

Use these numbers for exercises 7 and 8:   3.7   0.196   3.07   0.02   0.5

7. Order the numbers from least to greatest. _____________________

8. Order the numbers from greatest to least. _____________________

Choose the correct number from the box at the right.

918	300.15	87.8
88.7	176.9	40.287
40,287	91.8	30,015

9. three hundred and fifteen hundredths _______

10. eighty-eight and seven tenths _______

11. forty and two hundred eighty-seven thousandths _______

12. ninety-one and eight tenths _______

Solve.

13. What is the perimeter, in centimeters, of the figure below?

Perimeter = _____________________

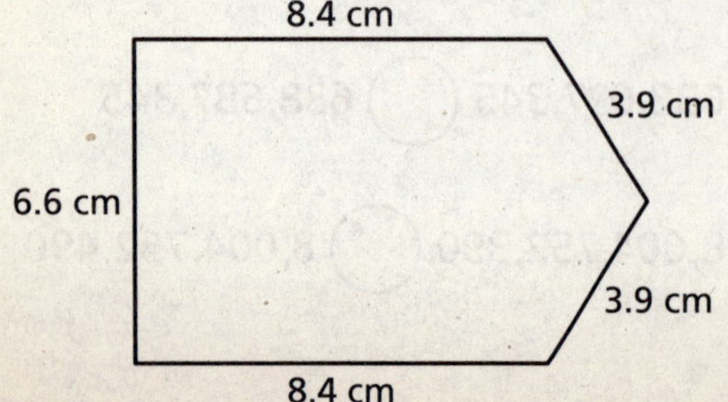

    Use Place Value

Homework

Use the number 724,062.581 for each exercise.

1. Increase the number by 0.007. _______________

2. Decrease the number by 100,000. _______________

3. Add 8 in the hundreds place. _______________

4. Subtract 2 from the hundredths place. _______________

Copy each exercise. Then add or subtract.

5. $37 + 45¢ = ______   **6.** $82.06 + 25¢ = ______   **7.** 59¢ + $4.23 = ______

8. 9 m + 0.05 m = ______   **9.** 6.4 m + 0.07 m = ______   **10.** 5 m + 0.08 m = ______

11. 231 + 0.26 = ______   **12.** 46.08 + 0.97 = ______   **13.** 92.24 + 3.6 = ______

Show your work.

Solve.

14. Olivia is buying a jacket that costs $84. The sales tax
that will be added to the cost of the jacket is $4.65.
What is the total cost of the jacket?

____

Name _______________________ **Date** _______________________

Remembering

Compare. Write = (is equal to) or ≠ (is not equal to).

1. 6.003 ◯ 6.03   **2.** 106.72 ◯ 106.9   **3.** 98.07 ◯ 98.070

4. 5 ◯ 5.000   **5.** 0.14 ◯ 0.104   **6.** 0.1 ◯ 0.100

7. 0.000 ◯ 0   **8.** 11.0 ◯ 11   **9.** 5.020 ◯ 5.002

10. 18.6 ◯ 18.60   **11.** 0.2 ◯ 2.0   **12.** 7.04 ◯ 7.40

Use the number 427,389.106 for exercises 13–20.

13. The digit 7 is in the _______________ place.

14. The digit 1 is in the _______________ place.

15. What digit is in the hundreds place? _______________

16. What digit is in the thousandths place? _______________

17. The digit 9 is in the _______________ place.

18. What digit is in the ten thousands place? _______________

19. The digit 4 is in the _______________ place.

20. Write the number using words.

____

____

Use the digits 6, 9, and 1 for exercises 21–24. Use each digit once.

21. Write the greatest three-digit whole number. _______________

22. Write the smallest three-digit whole number. _______________

23. Write the greatest three-digit decimal number in hundredths. _______________

24. Write the smallest three-digit decimal number in tenths. _______________

   Add Whole Numbers and Decimals

Name   Date

Homework

Add each pair of numbers.

1. $80{,}615.405 + 3{,}468.27$

2. $512{,}019 + 6{,}478.084$

3. $2.765 + 19.6529$

4. $0.825 + 647.52$

5. $10{,}856.29 + 9{,}753.779$

6. $901{,}728.6 + 7{,}286.903$

Use the number $4,697,385.65 for exercises 7–12.

7. Add 3 million dollars. ________________

8. Subtract 5 thousand dollars. ________________

9. Add 20 dollars. ________________

10. Take $10,000 away. ________________

11. Add 2 dimes. ________________

12. Subtract 1 penny. ________________

Remembering

Solve for each unknown.

1. $(5 \cdot 8) \div 4 = c$ **2.** $d = 72 \div (9 - 1)$ **3.** $a = (5 \times 6) - 17$

$c =$ _______ $d =$ _______ $a =$ _______

4. $(35 + 7) \div 7 = r$ **5.** $21 \cdot s = 0$ **6.** $3t = (4 + 5) \times 3$

$r =$ _______ $s =$ _______ $t =$ _______

Solve.

Emilio is planting a garden, but he has mixed up the seeds. The seeds now need to be sorted. He has a book that tells him the lengths of different seeds. The lengths are shown below.

Emilio doesn't completely understand decimal numbers. You can help him by listing the seeds from longest to shortest. Then Emilio will be able to identify and sort his seeds.

Sizes of Seeds   **Seeds in Order of Size**

Tomato 0.3 cm   Longest   **7.** _______________

Pumpkin 1.25 cm   **8.** _______________

Watermelon 0.9 cm   **9.** _______________

Carrot 0.15 cm   **10.** _______________

Corn 0.75 cm   **11.** _______________

Eggplant 0.25 cm   Shortest   **12.** _______________

Write the perimeter and the area of the figure below.

13. Perimeter = _______________

14. Area = _______________

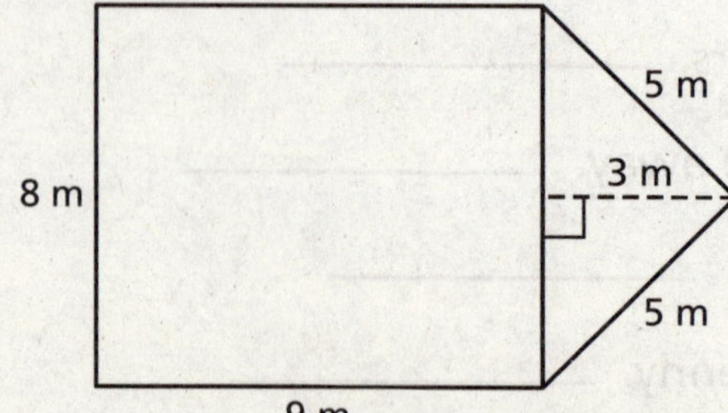

Homework

Copy each exercise. Then subtract.

1. 6,000 − 348 = ______   **2.** 7,364 − 937 = ______   **3.** 50,821 − 3,617 = ______

4. 720.95 − 286.4 = ______   **5.** 18,652 − 4.31 = ______   **6.** 350.6 − 176.54 = ______

Solve.   *Show your work.*

7. Ahmad had a piece of rope that was 7.14 meters long. He cut off 0.095 meters to practice making knots. What was the length of the rope after the cut?

____

8. Natasha has a large collection of books. The thickest book measures 4.9 centimeters. The thinnest book measures 1.8 centimeters. What is the difference in thicknesses of those two books?

____

9. Yoshi saved $1,238.46 for a vacation in Mexico. While in Mexico, she spent $975. What amount of money did Yoshi not spend?

____

10. Tarantulas are one of the largest spiders on Earth. A tarantula can grow to be about 6.8 centimeters long. A spitting spider can grow to be about 0.9 centimeters long. About how much longer are the largest tarantulas than the largest spitting spiders?

____

Remembering

Circle the value in each group that is not equivalent to the other values.

1. 9.050   9.05   09.050   0.950   09.05

2. 1.410   1.041   01.41   1.4100   01.410

3. 2.650   02.65   2.605   2.65   02.650

Write each decimal number.

4. 2 thousand and 8 tenths _____________

5. 31 thousand and 57 hundredths _____________

6. 94 thousand, 631 and 7 thousandths _____________

7. six million and five hundredths _____________

Write each amount as a decimal number.

8. 6 tenths _______

9. 4 thousandths _______

10. 2 hundredths _______

11. $\frac{18}{100}$ _______

12. $9\frac{3}{10}$ _______

13. $\frac{26}{1,000}$ _______

14. 73 hundredths _______

15. 1 tenth _______

16. 8 thousandths _______

Calculate the perimeter (P) of each figure in *feet*.

17. 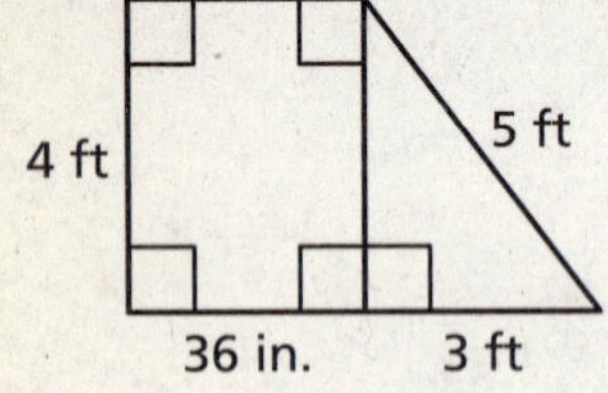

P = _____________

18. 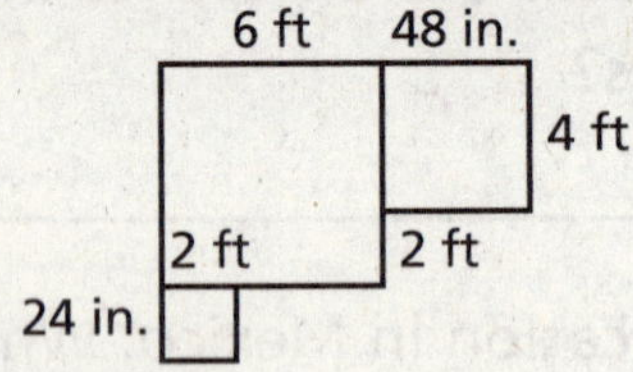

P = _____________

19. 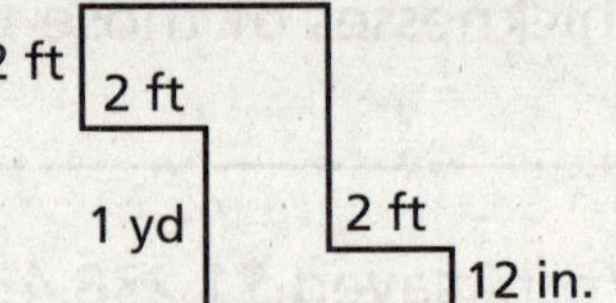

P = _____________

Solve the Factor Puzzles.

20. 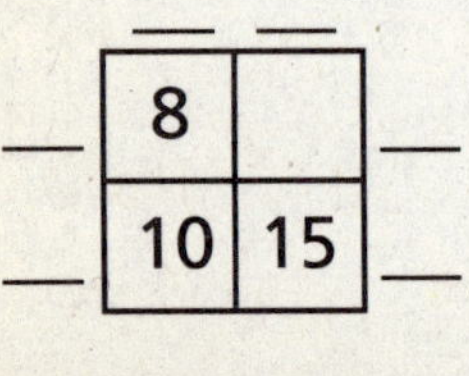

21.

22.

Subtract Whole and Decimal Numbers

Name _______________________   **Date** _______________

Homework

Use the data in the table to answer the questions that follow.

Lakefront Summer Concerts

Musical Group	Date	Audience Size	Ticket Sales
Wink	May 5	47,591	$475,910
Fred's Garage	May 26	59,985	$599,850
The Insiders	June 8	51,872	$518,720
The Beat Masters	June 19	43,469	$434,690
Paparazzi	June 27	56,327	$563,270

1. Which musical group entertained the largest audience?   _Show your work._

____

2. How many total people were in the audience at the concerts during May? During June?

May ____

June ____

3. For each concert, 60,000 tickets could have been sold. How many tickets were not sold when The Insiders performed? When Paparazzi performed?

The Insiders _______________________________

Paparazzi _________________________________

4. What amount of money represents the total ticket sales for May? for June?

May ____

June ____

5. What pattern do you see between the audience size and the ticket sales? _______________________________

6. What does this tell you about the cost of the tickets?

____

Remembering

Use the number 24,168.05 for exercises 1–6.

1. Increase the number by 1,000. ________________

2. Write the number with 2 fewer tens. ________________

3. Decrease the number by 3 hundredths. ________________

4. Write the number with 5 more ten thousands.

____

5. Write the number with 9 more in the tenths place.

____

6. Increase the number by 500. ________________

**Use the decimal numbers below to answer the questions
that follow.**

  0.2698   2.698   0.02698   0.26980   26.980

7. Which number is the least? ________________

8. Which number is the greatest? ________________

9. Which two numbers are equivalent? ________________

Write the equivalent measurement.

10. 36 in. = ________ ft   11. 24 ft = ________ yd   12. 36 in. = ________ yd

13. 2 yd = ________ in.   14. 4 ft = ________ in.   15. 8 yd = ________ ft

Calculate the perimeter (*P*) and the area (*A*) of each rectangle.

16.
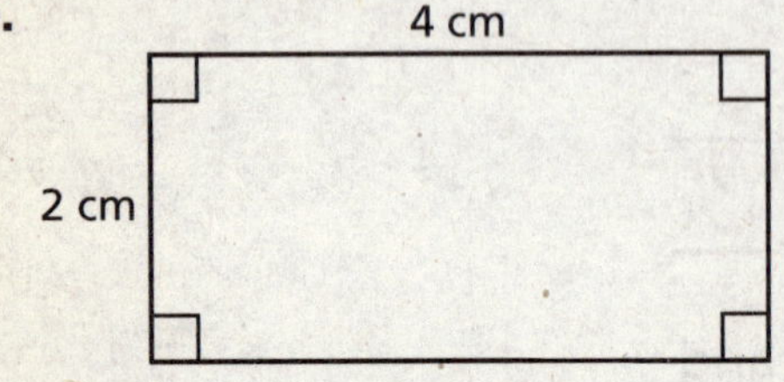

17.
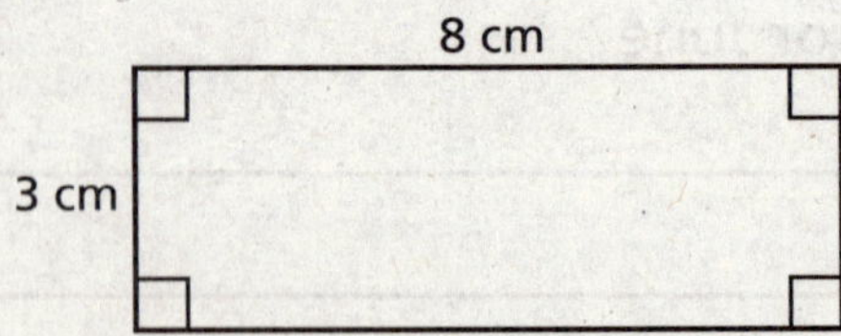

$P =$ ________________ $P =$ ________________

$A =$ ________________ $A =$ ________________

Homework

Use the Commutative Property to solve for n.

1. $26{,}184 + 1{,}546 = 1{,}546 + n$

$n =$ _______

2. $17.39 + 12.58 = 12.58 + n$

$n =$ _______

Regroup the numbers using the Associative Property. Then add.

3. $(389 + 700) + 300 =$

____

4. $1.02 + (0.98 + 4.87) =$

____

Use the Distributive Property to rewrite each problem so it has only two factors. Then solve.

5. $(8 \times 700) + (8 \times 300) =$

____

6. $(25 \times 9) + (75 \times 9) =$

____

Group the numbers to make the addition easier. Then add.

7.	8.	9.	10.
20,000	10,000	10.75	1.600
70,000	25,000	10.4	1.200
30,000	89,000	10.25	1.200
68,000	75,000	10.57	+ 1.479
+ 80,000	+ 90,000	+ 10.6	

Subtract.

11. $\$182.09 - 37¢ =$ _________

12. $\$5{,}287.32 - 59¢ =$ _________

13. $\$362 - 48¢ =$ _________

14. $6 \text{ m} - 0.03 \text{ m} =$ _________

15. $8 \text{ dm} - 0.5 \text{ dm} =$ _________

16. $4 \text{ m} - 0.032 \text{ m} =$ _________

Remembering

Use these decimal numbers to answer the questions that follow.

68.70   6.870   6.087   6.87   0.6870

1. Which number is the least? ___________________

2. Which number is the greatest? ___________________

3. Which two numbers are equivalent? ___________________

Compare. Write >, <, or =.

4. 0.09 $\bigcirc$ 0.7   5. 0.30 $\bigcirc$ 0.3   6. 0.86 $\bigcirc$ 0.7

7. 0.461 $\bigcirc$ 0.416   8. 1.9 $\bigcirc$ 0.83   9. 0.5 $\bigcirc$ 0.500

10. 1.26 $\bigcirc$ 12.6   11. 7.00 $\bigcirc$ 7   12. 2 $\bigcirc$ 0.2

Solve.   *Show your work.*

13. What is the greatest 3-digit whole number you can make using the digits 5, 8, and 2 once? What is the least 3-digit whole number you can make?

____

14. What is the smallest decimal number you can make using the digits 5, 0, 8, and 2 once?

____

15. Cherise is growing a tomato plant for her science project. At the end of the first week, the plant was 4.7 cm tall. During the second week, the plant had grown 0.9 cm. How tall was the plant at the end of the second week?

____

Use the information in each problem to make a pictograph.

1. The Horizon Book Company needs a pictograph showing the number of books sold this year. Using the information shown, make a pictograph. Give your graph a title and a key.

Children	500,000
Adults	700,000

Books for Children	
Books for Adults	
	Key: ________

2. The Melodic Music Company needs a pictograph showing the number of CDs sold this year. Using the information shown, make a pictograph. Remember to include the title and the key.

Rock	40,000
Country	30,000
Jazz	15,000
Classical	5,000

Rock	
Country	
Jazz	
Classical	
	Key: ________

3. Ask 2 questions about your pictograph for problem 2 and then answer them.

____

____

____

Remembering

Answer each question about the decimal numbers.

58.76   5.876   0.05876   5.8760   0.5876

1. Which number is the smallest?

____

2. Which number is the greatest?

____

3. Which two numbers are equivalent?

____

Write each number.

4. seven tenths

____

5. thirty million

____

6. eight hundredths

____

7. four million one

____

8. forty-five thousand six

____

9. seven hundred fifty thousand ten

____

10. eighty thousand twenty-nine

____

11. two thousandths

____

**For each measurement, write an equivalent length in
decimeters (dm), centimeters (cm), and millimeters (mm).**

12. 13.74 m   _________ dm   _________ cm   _________ mm

13. 0.85 m   _________ dm   _________ cm   _________ mm

Homework

Name   Date

Round to the nearest ten.

1. 62 ________   2. 91 ________

Round to the nearest thousand.

3. 3,205 ________   4. 8,500 ________

Round to the nearest hundred.

5. 493 ________   6. 1,580 ________

Round to the nearest 10 thousand.

7. 50,926 ________   8. 75,612 ________

Decide whether a *safe* or an *ordinary* estimate is needed. Then estimate to find each answer.

Show your work.

9. Amy has 5,805 large beads and 3,950 small beads. About how many more large beads than small beads does Amy have?

10. Lincoln School has 54 fifth-graders, and Elm School has 38 fifth-graders. The two schools will have a party together. Each fifth-grade student will get a balloon. About how many balloons should the teachers buy?

11. In a parking garage, there are 598 cars and 214 vans. About how many vehicles are in the parking garage altogether?

12. A sports shop sold $15,679 worth of roller blades and $16,231 worth of skateboards this year. About how much money did the shop make on these two items?

Remembering

At the county fair each August, there is a contest to see who can grow the tallest sunflower. Below is a table that shows how tall each sunflower plant is.

1. Make a list showing whose plants got first place, second place, and third place.

   Sunflower Growers

Arturo	4.781 m
Jan	5.935 m
Shen	6.105 m
Max	6.20 m
Madison	5.92 m
Alex	5.915 m

   First Place ______________

   Second Place ______________

   Third Place ______________

Solve.

2. Michaela, Simone, and Veronica want to buy T-shirts for the science club. If the club treasurer gives them $35.00, and they spend $27.50 on the T-shirts, how much money will they have left?

   Show your work.

   ____

3. Michaela, Simone, and Veronica want to buy special glitter paint with the leftover money. The paint is on sale. They can buy 3 tubes for $6.00. Do they have enough money to buy 3 tubes of paint? If so, how much money will they have left?

   ____

Find the area of each right triangle.

4. 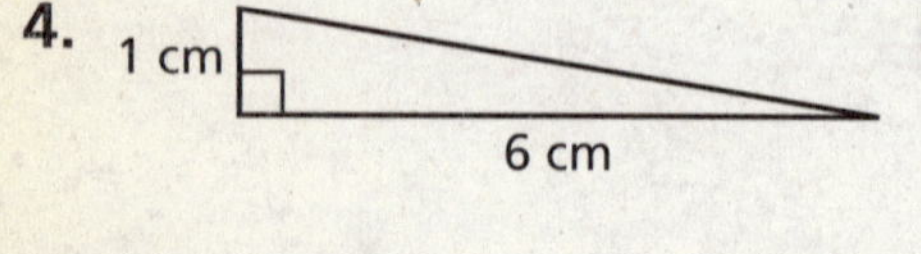

   ____

5.

   ____

6. 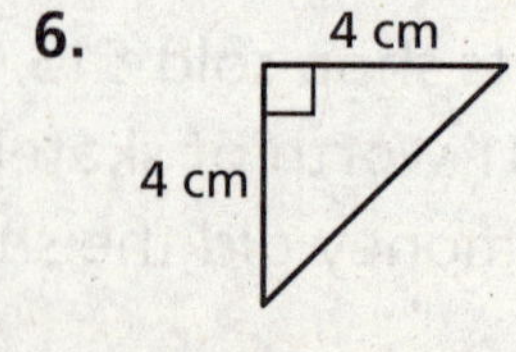

   ____

Name _______________________   **Date** _______________________

Homework

A forest ranger estimated the number of trees in the forest and made this bar graph.

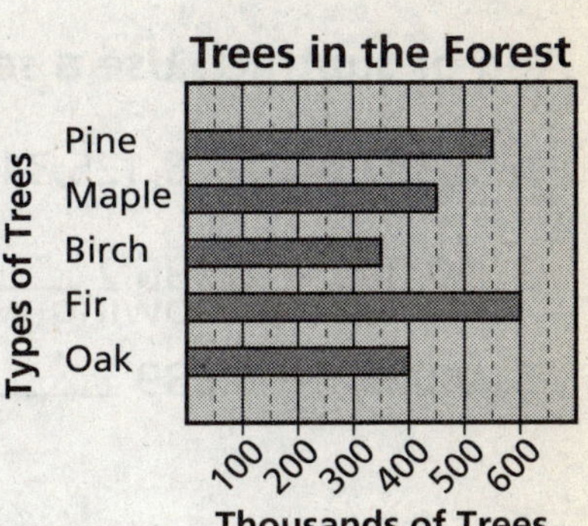

1. About how many maple trees are in the forest?

____

2. About how many fir and pine trees are there altogether?

____

3. About how many more oak trees are there than birch trees?

____

4. Write an estimate of the total number of trees in the forest.

____

Make a bar graph.

The table below shows an estimate of the number of cats, dogs, and birds kept as pets in the United States.

5. Make a bar graph to show these data. Make your own scale.

Cats	59,000,000
Dogs	53,000,000
Birds	13,000,000

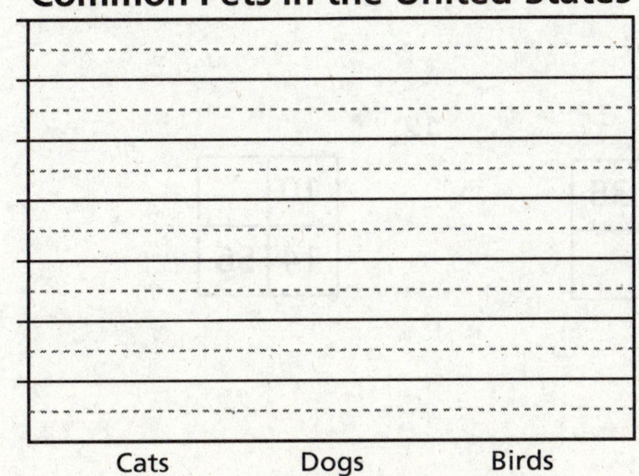

Remembering

Add or subtract. Use a separate sheet of paper.

1. 2,387,046 + 6,125,348 ____________

2. 38.567 + 4.286 ____________

3. 50,000 − 8,936.2 ____________

4. 5.004 + 0.38 ____________

5. 0.0852 − 0.039 ____________

6. 5.004 − 0.38 ____________

Use the pictograph to solve.

Seashells Collected

Meg	🐚 🐚 🐚
Kelly	🐚 🐚 🐚 🐚 🐚 🐚
Jon	🐚 🐚 🐚 🐚
Carol	🐚 🐚
Roberto	🐚 🐚 🐚 🐚

🐚 = 50 seashells

7. Who has more seashells than Meg?

____

8. How many more seashells did Jon collect than Carol?

____

9. How many seashells did Kelly collect?

____

Solve the Factor Puzzles.

10.

	21	42
		30

11.

24	36
6	

12.

10	
14	56

Bar Graphs and Rounding

Name _______________________   **Date** _______________

Homework

1. Round to the nearest whole number.

   a. 8.36 _______

   b. 18.7 _______

2. Round to the nearest hundredth.

   a. 58.635 _______

   b. 7.214 _______

3. Round to the nearest tenth.

   a. 24.316 _______

   b. 5.23 _______

4. Round to the nearest thousandth.

   a. 7.1488 _______

   b. 38.0769 _______

Copy and estimate each sum or difference.

5. $46.78 − $18.55

6. 12.3 + 4.7

7. 9.586 + 3.097

Solve.

Show your work.

8. A decimal number changed to 23.7 after it was rounded. Give a decimal number that is less than 23.7 and another that is greater than 23.7 that each round to 23.7. Explain to what place each number was rounded.

____

____

9. When Marla rounded 19.95 to the nearest tenth, she found the number changed to 20. Is this correct? Explain.

____

10. Peter decided that the total of a $24.55 pair of jeans and a $12.25 shirt was $26.80. Was Peter's answer reasonable? Explain why or why not.

____

11. Biruk wants to buy a book for $15.25 and a book for $4.85. He wants to pay with one $20 bill. Use estimation to decide if this is reasonable. Explain to what place value to round for an estimate that is useful in this situation.

____

____

Remembering

Add or subtract.

1. $41{,}253{,}270 + 6{,}050$

2. $14{,}365{,}024 + 7{,}840{,}993$

3. $5{,}000{,}000 - 563{,}000$

4. $35{,}789{,}630 - 2{,}894$

5. $83{,}918.7 + 605.357$

6. $10{,}250 - 4{,}200.24$

7. $9{,}473.2 + 851.69$

8. $756.42 - 94.51$

Use the Commutative Property to solve for n.

9. $98{,}551 + 2{,}841 = 2{,}841 + n$

$n =$ _________

10. $65.18 + 75.43 = 75.43 + n$

$n =$ _________

Use the Associative Property to regroup the numbers. Then add.

11. $(496 + 800) + 200$

____

12. $2.25 + (0.75 + 8.57)$

____

Solve.

Show your work.

13. Nathaniel says his string project uses 7.5 ft of string. Kara says her project uses 7.52 ft of string. Who used the least amount of string? Explain how you know.

____

14. Last month, Myles ran 14.55 miles while training for a marathon. Frances ran 0.6 miles farther than Myles. How far did Frances run last month?

____

   Round and Estimate with Decimal Numbers

Name ___________________________   **Date** ___________

Homework

Use the line graph below to answer the questions that follow.

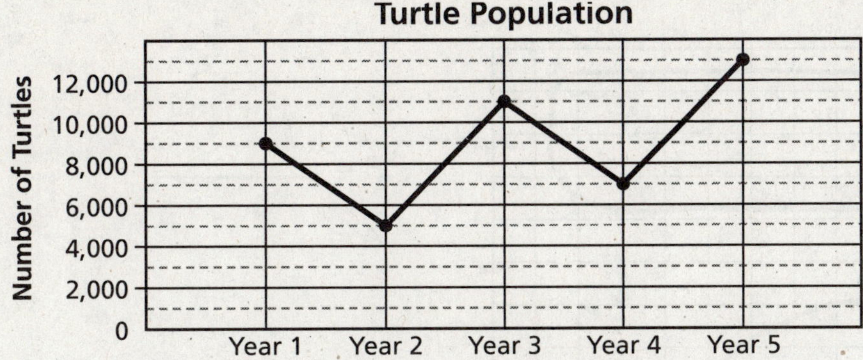

1. The graph shows the turtle population at the end of each year during a 5-year period. What was the turtle population in Year 4? ________________

2. How much greater was the population in Year 1 than in Year 2? ________________

3. Which year represents the greatest turtle population? What was the population that year?

   ____

Make a line graph.

4. The table at the right shows a store's inventory of kites at the end of 4 months. Make a graph below to show an estimate of the number of kites at the end of each month. Make your own scale and title.

   ____

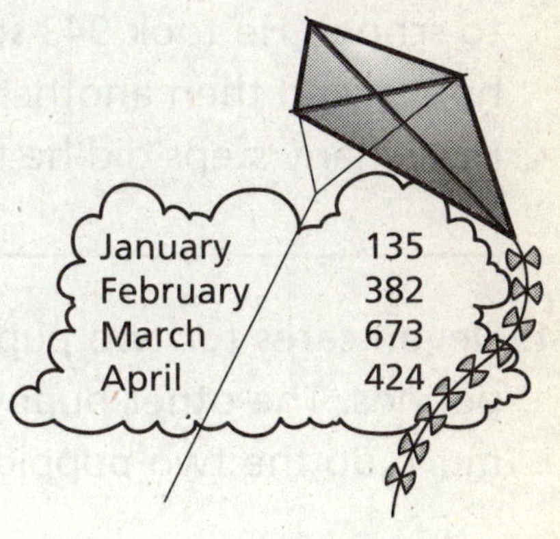

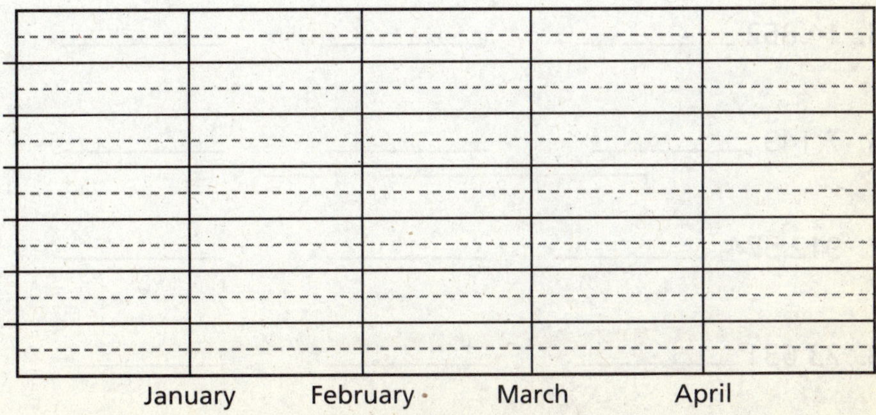

Remembering

Estimate the area and perimeter of each figure. Each side of each grid square represents 1 cm.

1.

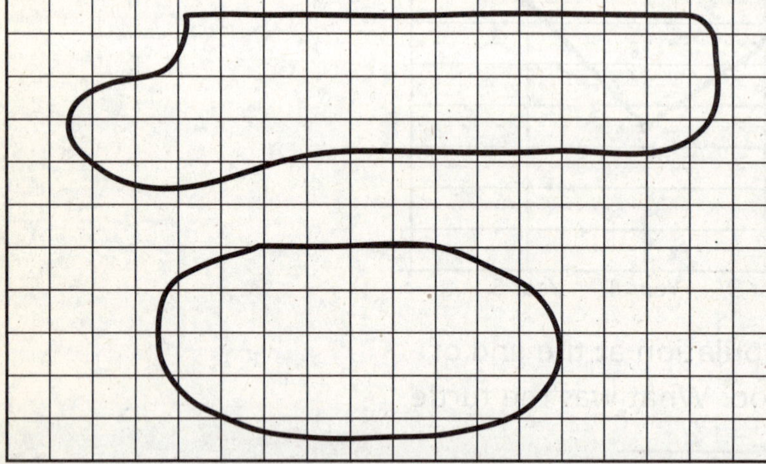

P = _________

A = _________

2.

P = _________

A = _________

Solve.

Show your work.

3. Chris counted the number of steps he took on his way to school. He took 943 steps to get to his friend's house, and then another 1,208 steps to get to school. How many steps did he take altogether?

____

4. Devon cares for two puppies. One puppy weighs 8.54 pounds. The other puppy weighs 12.39 pounds. How much do the two puppies weigh altogether?

____

Round each given decimal number to the nearest whole number, tenth, and hundredth.

5. 14.852 _________   _________   _________

6. 7.149 _________   _________   _________

7. 912.574 _________   _________   _________

8. 23.631 _________   _________   _________

Homework

Jamal made a line graph to show the weekly
growth of a flower he planted from a seed.

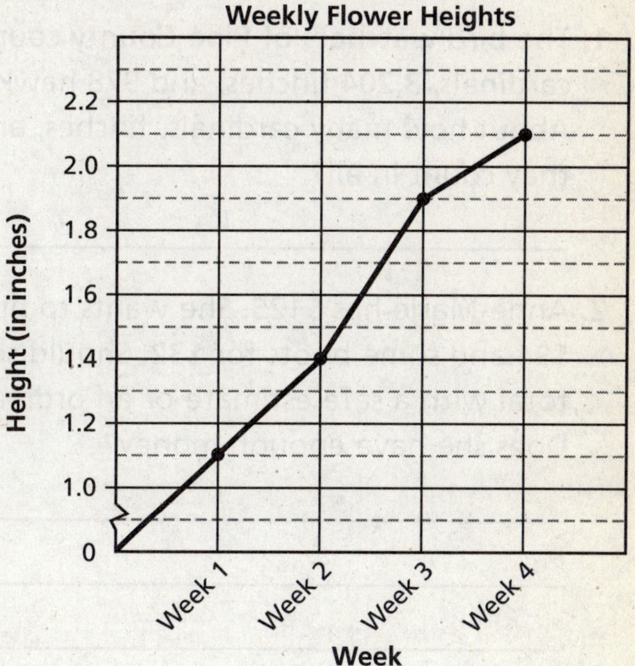

1. How much did the flower grow
   by Week 1?

   ____

2. How much did the flower grow
   between week 3 and week 4?

   ____

3. The flower reached its maximum
   height on Week 4. What is the
   tallest this flower will grow?

   ____

4. Between which two weeks did
   the flower grow the most?

   ____

The table shows the amount of rainfall this month in 4
different cities.

5. Make a bar graph showing this information. Remember
   to give your graph a title and a scale.

Chester	0.20 cm
Creekside	0.10 cm
Merton	0.05 cm
Warner	0.25 cm

Chester   Creekside   Merton   Warner

Remembering

Estimate.

Show your work.

1. The bird watchers of Pine County counted 2,956 cardinals, 3,204 finches, and 978 hawks this summer. About how many cardinals, finches, and hawks did they count in all?

____

2. Anne-Marie has $125. She wants to buy a jacket for $94 and some boots for $32. Should she estimate the total with a safe estimate or an ordinary estimate? Does she have enough money?

____

____

____

3. The Lightfoot Library has 31,823 books, but 9,625 are checked out right now. About how many books are still on the shelves?

____

4. A toothbrush factory made 2,461,200 electric toothbrushes and 5,847,500 regular toothbrushes this week. About how many toothbrushes did the factory make in all?

____

Write a decimal equivalent for each fraction.

5. $\dfrac{76}{100}$ 6. $\dfrac{349}{100}$ 7. $\dfrac{9}{100}$ 8. $\dfrac{5}{100}$ 9. $\dfrac{2}{10}$

_______   _______   _______   _______   _______

10. How many congruent isosceles triangles are inside the regular octagon? __________

11. What is the area of each triangle? __________

12. What is the area of the octagon? __________

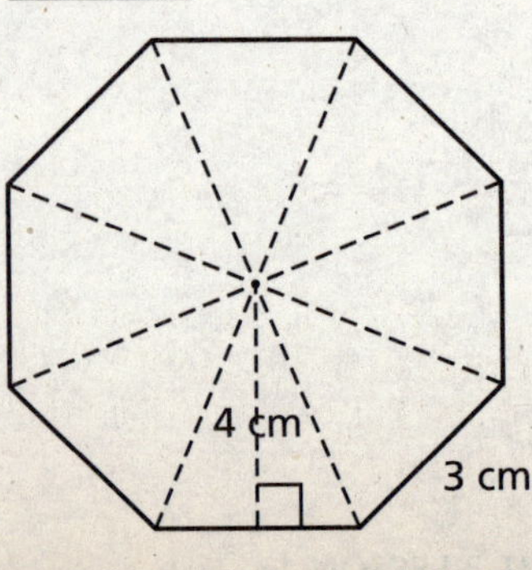

Graphs With Decimal Numbers

Homework

In your Math Journal or on a sheet of paper, write a word problem for each situation and answer the questions.

Situation 1

1. Write a word problem that represents a change situation.

2. Did you write a change plus or a change minus situation?

3. Is your situation an unknown result, unknown change, or unknown start?

Situation 2

4. Write a word problem that represents a collection situation.

5. Does your situation include an unknown total or an unknown partner?

6. Does you situation represent a take apart, put together, or no action situation?

Situation 3

7. Write a word problem that represents a comparison situation.

8. Does your situation have an unknown difference or an unknown quantity?

Solve these comparison problems.

Show your work.

9. Camille collected 13 shells from the beach. Her friend Sarah collected 10 times as many. How many shells did Sarah collect? ______________________________

10. Last week, Armando read 285 pages of a book. This week, he read 196 pages. How many fewer pages did he read this week? ______________________________

11. The Eiffel Tower in Paris is 300 meters tall. It is 253.5 meters taller than the Statue of Liberty. How tall is the Statue of Liberty? ______________________________

Name ______________________ **Date** ______________________

Remembering

Add or subtract. Use a separate sheet of paper.

1. 17,092 − 3,746 = ______________________

2. 657.92 + 53.035 = ______________________

3. 62.004 − 48.65 = ______________________

4. 831.5 − 46.75 = ______________________

5. 190.98 + 256.3 = ______________________

6. 41.003 − 7.02 = ______________________

7. 24 − 0.04 = ______________________

8. 9.72 + 31 = ______________________

**Use the Distributive Property to rewrite the expressions.
Then multiply.**

9. (7 × 600) + (7 × 400)

____

10. (30 × 6) + (70 × 6)

____

Solve.

Show your work.

11. Antonia bought 6.25 yards of fabric for two school projects.
She used 3.75 yards for the first project. She needs at least
3 yards for her second project. Does Antonia have enough
fabric? Explain how you can use estimation to find your answer.

____

____

12. Logan has 5.33 pounds of flour in his bakery. He bought
11.59 pounds more flour. He needs at most 16 pounds of
flour. Does Logan have enough flour? Explain how you
can use estimation to find your answer.

____

____

Classify Word Problems

Name   Date

Homework

Write a situation equation and a solution equation for each problem. Then solve the problem.

1. At the chicken ranch this morning there were 7,149 chicks. Later today some more chicks hatched. Now the ranch has 8,945 chicks. How many new chicks hatched today?

   _____________ _____________ _____________
   Situation Equation   Solution Equation   Answer

2. The library had a large collection of books. Then the librarian ordered 2,000 more books. Now there are 12,358 books. How many books were there at the start?

   _____________ _____________ _____________
   Situation Equation   Solution Equation   Answer

3. Rosa's parents collected $682 at their yard sale. They paid her for helping out that day. Now they have $662.25. How much money did Rosa's parents pay her?

   _____________ _____________ _____________
   Situation Equation   Solution Equation   Answer

4. Marco sells caramel apples at the state fair. Today he sold 957 apples, and now he has 1,062 left to sell. How many caramel apples did Marco begin with?

   _____________ _____________ _____________
   Situation Equation   Solution Equation   Answer

Find the unknown number. Use mental math if you can.

5. $80{,}000 + r = 82{,}000$ $r =$ _________

6. $0.005 + g = 0.105$ $g =$ _________

7. $r + 655 = 2{,}655$ $t =$ _________

8. $b + 0.36 = 25.36$ $b =$ _________

9. $6{,}500 = 7{,}000 - z$ $z =$ _________

10. $0.135 = 0.130 + c$ $c =$ _________

11. $f - 10{,}000 = 25{,}000$ $f =$ _________

12. $w - 2.5 = 0.3$ $w =$ _________

Remembering

Name the most sensible metric unit for each measurement.

1. The width of this button. 

____

2. The length of this pencil.

____

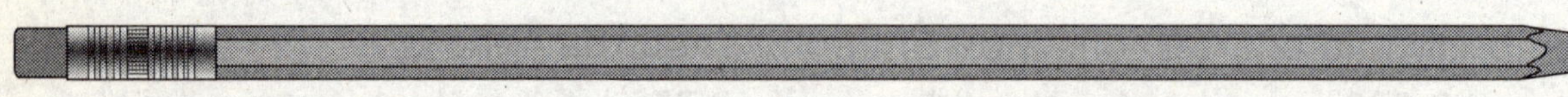

3. The length of an ant.

____

4. The longest dimension of your classroom.

____

Write a whole or decimal number for each word name.

5. eight tenths

____

7. five million, ten

____

9. two hundred forty thousand, twelve

____

6. twenty million

____

8. sixty-five thousand, four

____

10. six hundred four thousand

____

Use the bar graph at the right to answer the following questions.

11. How many angelfish are in the aquarium?

____

12. How many catfish and clown fish are there altogether?

____

Types of Fish in the Aquarium

     Situation and Solution Equations

Homework

Solve.   *Show your work.*

1. There are 476,092 fish in the city aquarium. That number of fish is 476,070 more fish than Nadia has in her aquarium. How many fish does Nadia have in her aquarium?

   ____

2. The Follett family traveled 2,145 miles this summer. They traveled 1,296 fewer miles than the Garcia family. How far did the Garcia family travel?

   ____

3. A 15-year-old boy built the largest house of cards on record. It was made of 15,714 cards. Today Michael built a house of cards that was made of 200 cards. How many more cards must he use to tie the record?

   ____

4. Maria wants to buy a new car. She will choose a green car or a silver car. The green car costs $16,898, and the silver car costs $1,059.75 less than the green car. What is the cost of the silver car?

   ____

5. A bakery has produced 5,285 loaves of bread so far this year. That number of loaves is 200 more loaves than the bakery produced last year. How many loaves of bread did the bakery produce last year?

   ____

Find the unknown number. Use mental math if you can.

6. $80{,}000 - q = 60{,}000$ $q =$ _______

7. $0.003 + p = 0.403$ $p =$ _______

8. $t - 8{,}500 = 9{,}000$ $t =$ _______

9. $b + 0.005 = 0.015$ $b =$ _______

10. $7{,}000{,}000 = 7{,}000{,}020 - z$ $z =$ _______

11. $37.96 = 39.96 - c$ $c =$ _______

12. $f - 986 = 12{,}000$ $f =$ _______

13. $w - 0.5 = 16$ $w =$ _______

Name   Date

Remembering

Write a situation equation and a solution equation for each problem. Then solve the problem.

1. There were 761 campers at a campground. After a number of campers went home, 659 campers remained at the campground. How many campers went home?

   ___________   ___________   ___________

   Situation Equation   Solution Equation   Answer

2. After 143 new students arrived at Elm Street School, the enrollment was 1,356 students. How many students were enrolled before the new students arrived?

   ___________   ___________   ___________

   Situation Equation   Solution Equation   Answer

3. April sold 200 stamps from her collection. Now she has 2,250 stamps. How many stamps were in her collection before the sale?

   ___________   ___________   ___________

   Situation Equation   Solution Equation   Answer

Round to the nearest thousand.

4. 4,195 ________   5. 9,947 ________

6. 14,861 ________   7. 21,253 ________

Round to the nearest million.

8. 7,956,122 ________   9. 2,305,472 ________

10. 19,037,513 ________   11. 31,894,567 ________

Complete.

12. 48 in. = ________ ft   13. 36 ft = ________ yd   14. 7 yd = ________ ft

15. 3 yd = ________ in.   16. 2 ft = ________ in.   17. 36 in. = ________ yd

      Comparison Problems

Name _______________________ **Date** _______________________

Homework

Complete one or more steps to solve each problem.   *Show your work.*

1. The regular price of an item is $9,985. The sale price of the item is $9,575. What is the difference between the sale price and the regular price of 10 items?

   ____

2. The Stein family plans to drive 125.7 miles to Middletown. They drive 62.5 miles before they have to go back 10.2 miles for something they leave behind at a restaurant. How far from Middletown is the restaurant?

   ____

3. A toy factory made 15,000 toys and packed them in boxes of 10 each. The factory loaded 1,275 boxes on a delivery truck. How many boxes of toys were not loaded on the truck?

   ____

If the problem below has too much information, cross out the extra information. If it has too little information, tell what information is missing and add some possible missing information. Then solve each problem.

4. Jillian has $125.67 saved for a stereo. The stereo costs $175 and a television costs $295. She babysat for 4 hours this weekend and earned $7 an hour. How much more does she need to buy the stereo?

   ____

   ____

5. Michael ran a marathon to raise money for his favorite charity. Each sponsor agreed to pay $2 for each mile that he runs. He found a total of 6 sponsors. How much money did he raise?

   ____

   ____

Remembering

Round to the nearest 10,000 and the nearest 1,000.

1. 11,287 _______ _______   **2.** 45,732 _______ _______

3. 9,674 _______ _______   **4.** 89,135 _______ _______

Solve.   *Show your work.*

5. Last year Paco's bonsai tree was 6.75 centimeters tall. Today it is 8.40 centimeters tall. How much has the tree grown?

____

6. This morning the temperature outside was 12.5°C. At noon it was 3.7 degrees warmer. What was the temperature at noon?

____

7. A tomato seed is about 0.295 centimeters long. A cucumber seed is about 0.38 centimeters long.

Which seed is shorter? _______________________________

How much shorter? _______________________________

8. The Harrisons' dining room table with the table extension is 2.55 meters long. Without the extension the table is 2.25 meters long.

How long is the extension? _______________________________

9. The perimeter of an equilateral triangle is 45 inches. A rectangle whose width is $\frac{1}{3}$ its length has a perimeter of 48 inches. Which figure has the *longest* side? Explain.

____

____

____

____

____

____

Homework

1. **Connections** Lorenzo is a realtor and wants to become a member of the Million Dollar Club. To do this he must have at least $1 million in sales. So far, he has sold three homes for $256,900, $373,100, and $284,400. How can you quickly tell if these sales will allow him to be a member? If they can't, how much more does he need in sales?

____

____

____

____

____

2. **Representation** Susan owns a card shop. She kept a record of the number of cards sold each month for one year. Then, she used a line graph to graph the data she collected. Explain what the line graph showed and how she might use the data.

____

____

____

____

____

____

____

____

3. **Communication** Hanna bought 4 pencils for 9¢ each, two notebooks for $1.58 each, and one pack of paper for $3.17 each. She paid with $10 and received $3.58 in change. Is the change correct? If not, identify the correct amount of change and why the error was made.

____

____

____

____

____

____

4. **Reasoning and Proof** Can you draw a square that has an area and a perimeter that are not the same, such as, an area of 16 m² and a perimeter of 20 m? Explain your answer.

____

____

____

____

____

____

Remembering

Use the number 149,578.324 for exercises 1–6.

1. Increase the number by 5 more hundredths.

   ____

2. Decrease the number by 1 hundred thousand.

   ____

3. Decrease the number by 4 tens.

   ____

4. Increase the number by one hundred thirteen thousandths.

   ____

Solve.

5. Last week, Jillian drove 113.4 miles and 49.67 miles.
   So far this week, she has driven 152.89 miles. How
   many more miles will she have to drive this week to
   equal the miles driven last week?

   ____

Write a situation equation and a solution equation. Then solve.

6. The charity held a banquet as a fundraiser. After paying
   $1,796 in expenses from the money collected, the charity
   has $4,853 left. How much did the charity collect in all
   at the party?

   ____________   ____________   ____________

   Situation Equation   Solution Equation   Answer

7. Skyler bought 214 more baseball cards at a flea market.
   He now has 567 baseball cards in his collection. How
   many baseball cards did he have before the purchase?

   ____________   ____________   ____________

   Situation Equation   Solution Equation   Answer

Homework

1. Use your ruler. Draw two lines that intersect. Label the lines and their point of intersection.

2. Name all the lines in your drawing.

   ____

3. Name four rays in your drawing.

   ____

4. Name four angles in your drawing.

   ____

5. Name two pairs of vertical angles formed by the intersecting lines below.

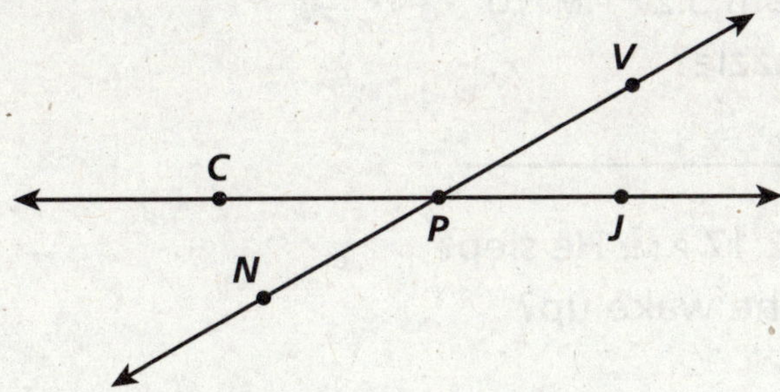

Use this diagram for exercises 6–9.

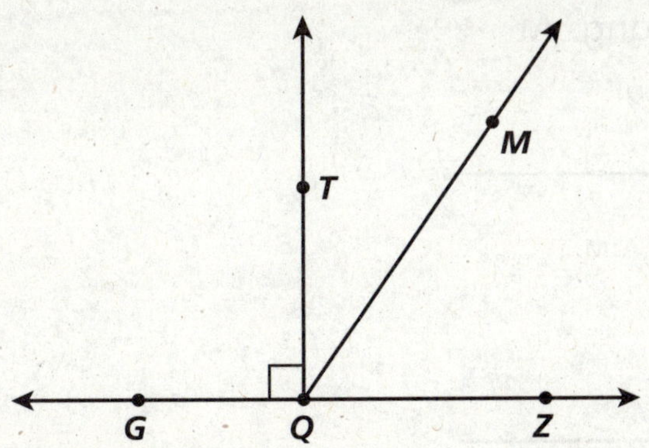

6. Which angles are complementary angles?

   ____

7. Which angles are supplementary angles?

   ____

8. Which angle is a straight angle?

   ____

9. Which angles are right angles?

   ____

Remembering

Solve.

1. $28 \div 4 =$ _____   2. $2 \times 9 =$ _____   3. $54 \div 6 =$ _____   4. $8 \times 0 =$ _____

5. $5 \times 5 =$ _____   6. $63 \div 7 =$ _____   7. $3 \times 4 =$ _____   8. $20 \div 5 =$ _____

9. $81 \div 9 =$ _____   10. $12 \times 1 =$ _____   11. $15 \div 3 =$ _____   12. $6 \times 5 =$ _____

13. $3 \times 7 =$ _____   14. $18 \div 2 =$ _____   15. $7 \times 6 =$ _____   16. $45 \div 9 =$ _____

17. $80 \div 8 =$ _____   18. $4 \times 8 =$ _____   19. $0 \div 4 =$ _____   20. $9 \times 1 =$ _____

21. Ah Lam and George worked on a puzzle from 5:27 P.M. to 7:11 P.M. How long did they work on the puzzle?

____

22. Deacon's baby brother began napping at 12:17 P.M. He slept for 2 hours and 12 minutes. What time did he wake up?

____

23. Rebecca and her friends finished watching a movie at 2:25 P.M. The movie was 1 hour and 43 minutes long. At what time did they start the movie?

____

24. The Diaz family left to visit with friends at 10:43 A.M. They arrived at their friends' home at 1:09 P.M. How long was the trip?

____

Homework

Complete each statement.

1. The total of the angle measures of a __________________
is always 180°.

2. The total of the angle measures of a __________________
is always 360°.

Write the measure of the unknown angle.

3.

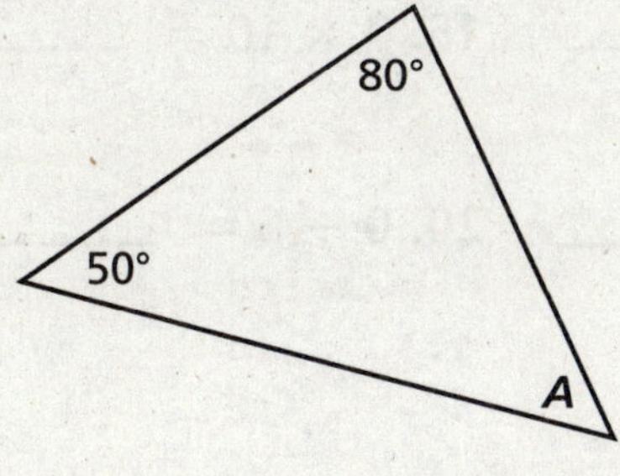

______

4.

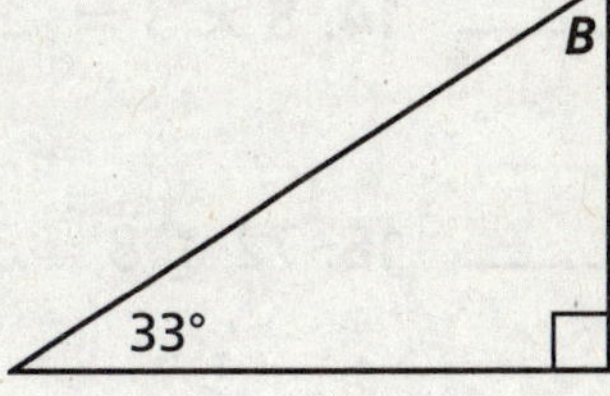

5.

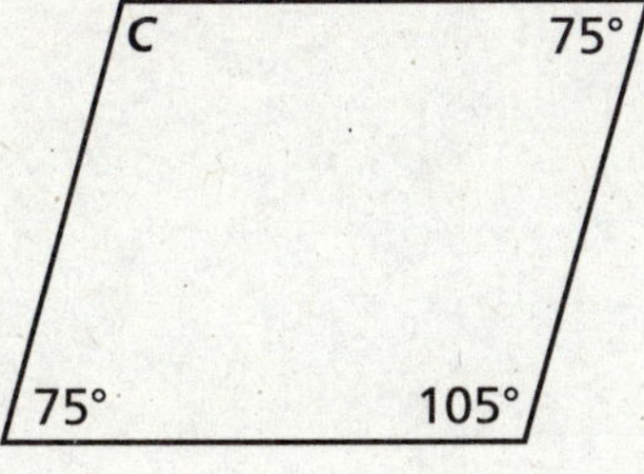

______

6.

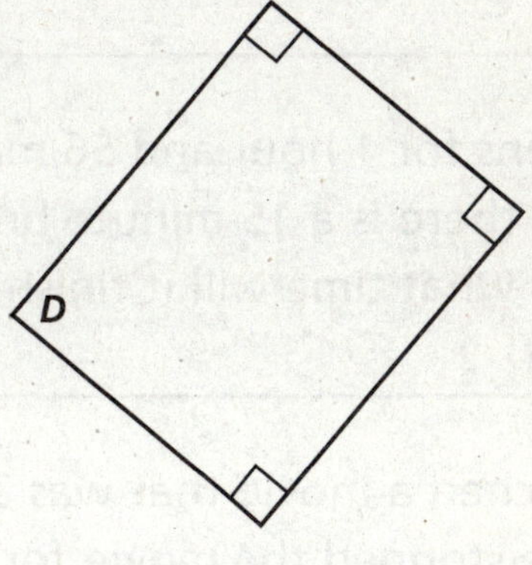

______

7. One angle measure in an isosceles triangle is 100°.
What is the measure of each of the other angles?

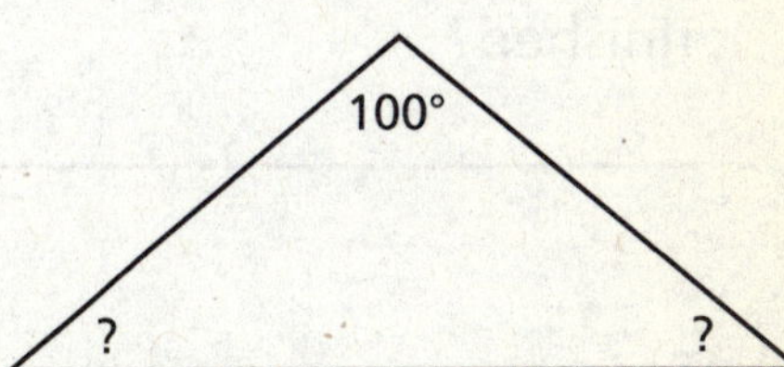

____

8. Two angle measures in a parallelogram are 80°.
What is the measure of each of the other angles?

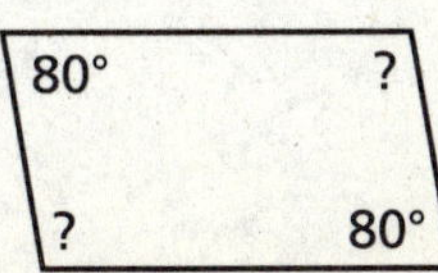

____

Name **Date**

Remembering

Solve.

1. 2 × 3 = _____   2. 77 ÷ 7 = _____   3. 8 × 6 = _____   4. 10 ÷ 1 = _____

5. 49 ÷ 7 = _____   6. 10 × 4 = _____   7. 4 ÷ 2 = _____   8. 7 × 0 = _____

9. 4 × 4 = _____   10. 64 ÷ 8 = _____   11. 1 × 3 = _____   12. 12 ÷ 3 = _____

13. 10 ÷ 2 = _____   14. 8 × 3 = _____   15. 6 ÷ 1 = _____   16. 2 × 10 = _____

17. 11 × 1 = _____   18. 72 ÷ 8 = _____   19. 7 × 5 = _____   20. 0 ÷ 6 = _____

21. The Smiths hiked a trail marked "2 hours and 30 minutes."
They took a 20-minute break. If they arrived at the end of
the trail at 5:15 P.M., at what time did they start their hike?

____

22. A play runs for 1 hour and 56 minutes. Part way through
the play, there is a 15-minute break. If the play started at
4:30 P.M., what time will it finish?

____

23. Kuri watched a movie that was 2 hours and 13 minutes
long. She stopped the movie for 17 minutes. If she started
watching at 11:30 A.M., at what time was her movie
finished?

____

    Polygons and Angles

Name _______________________ **Date** ____________

Homework

In each row, circle all of the figures that look congruent.

1.

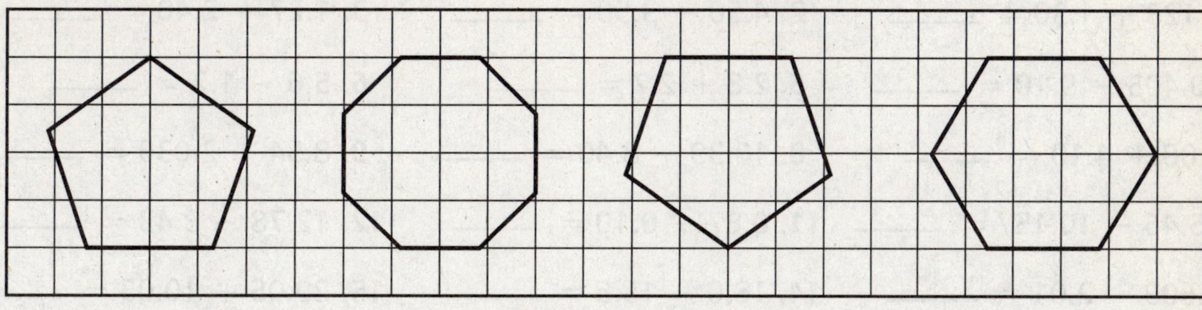

2.

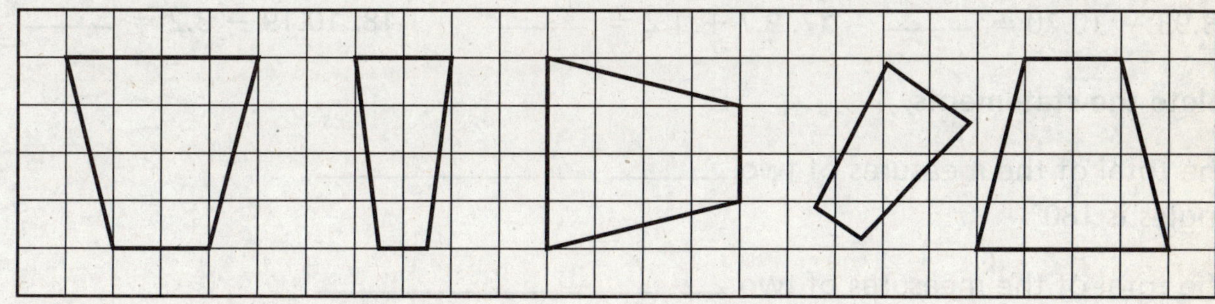

3.

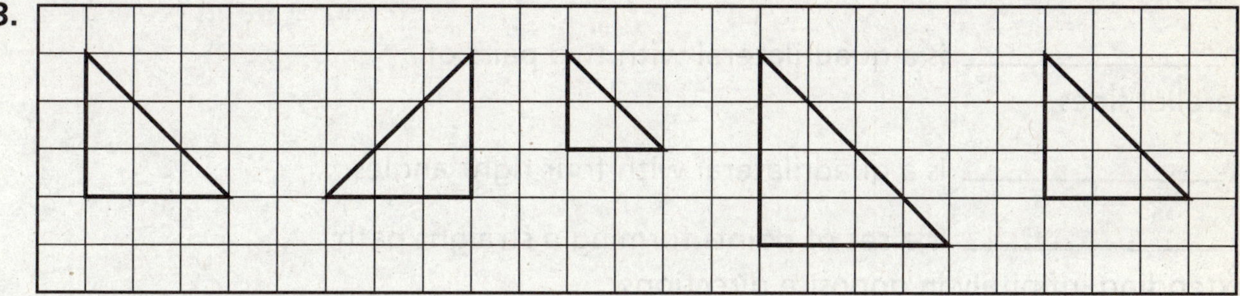

Write _always_, _sometimes_, or _never_ to complete each statement.

4. A quadrilateral ____________ has exactly two congruent angles.

5. A quadrilateral ____________ has exactly three congruent angles.

6. Draw a figure that is congruent to the figure below.

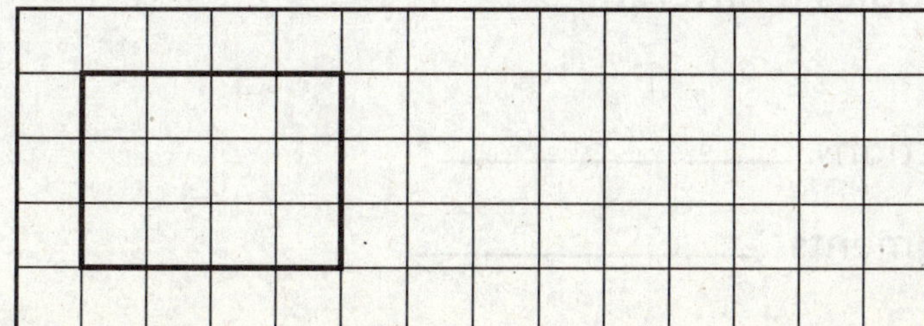

Remembering

Solve.

1. $0.123 + 1.30 =$ _____
2. $4.50 - 3.50 =$ _____
3. $1.27 + 2.40 =$ _____

4. $10.405 - 9.10 =$ _____
5. $2.8 + 2.7 =$ _____
6. $5.6 - 1.2 =$ _____

7. $3.08 + 4.10 =$ _____
8. $10.39 - 8.40 =$ _____
9. $8.54 + 2.039 =$ _____

10. $15.45 - 10.157 =$ _____
11. $0.87 + 0.10 =$ _____
12. $12.78 - 3.43 =$ _____

13. $7.609 - 2.01 =$ _____
14. $18.0 - 15.5 =$ _____
15. $20.05 + 10.05 =$ _____

16. $13.93 - 10.70 =$ _____
17. $9.7 + 1.2 =$ _____
18. $10.19 - 3.2 =$ _____

Complete the statements.

19. The total of the measures of two _____________________ angles is 180°.

20. The total of the measures of two _____________________ angles is 90°.

21. A _____________ is a quadrilateral with two pairs of parallel sides.

22. A _____________ is a quadrilateral with four right angles.

23. A _____________ is a set of points forming a straight path extending infinitely in opposite directions.

24. A _____________ is part of a line beginning at an endpoint and extending infinitely in one direction.

25. Two rays that share an endpoint form a(n) _____________.

Write true or false.

26. A quadrilateral can have each of 4 angles a different measure. _____________

27. A ray extends infinitely in both directions. _____________

28. A polygon has sides that are line segments. _____________

Homework

The measure of each shaded angle is given. Write the measure of each angle that is not shaded.

1.

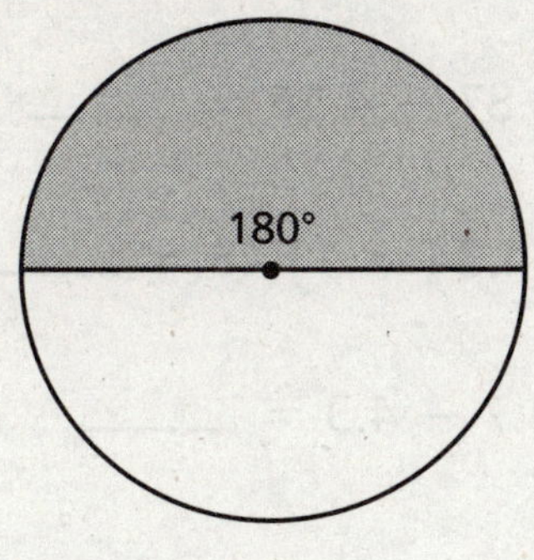

2.

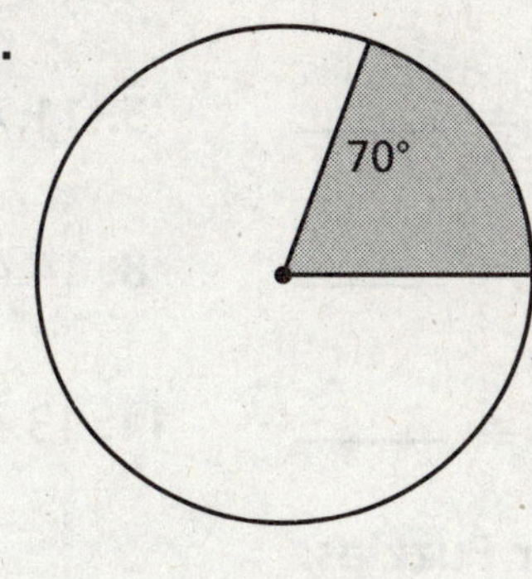

3.

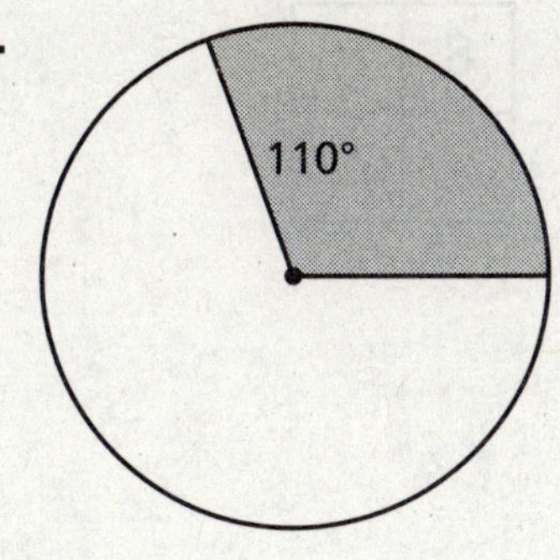

4.

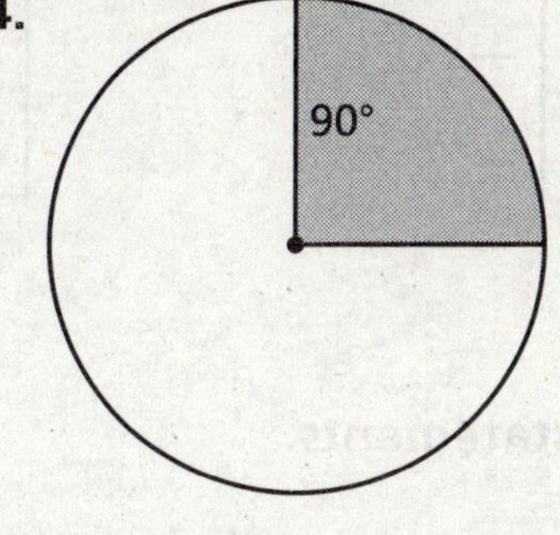

5. Draw the figure after a turn of 180° clockwise.

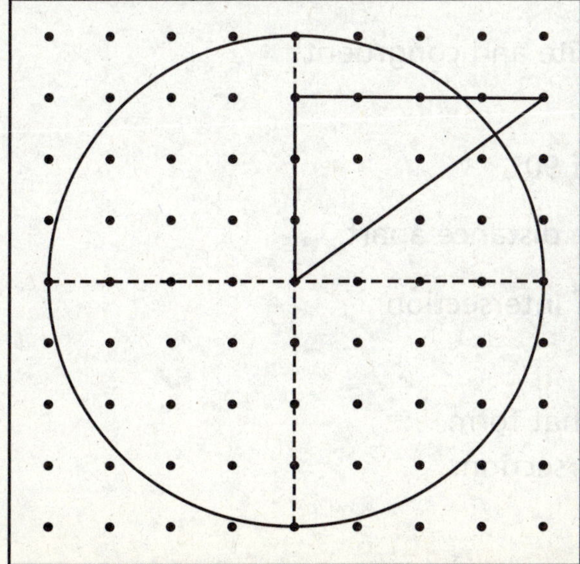

6. Draw the figure after a turn of 90° counterclockwise.

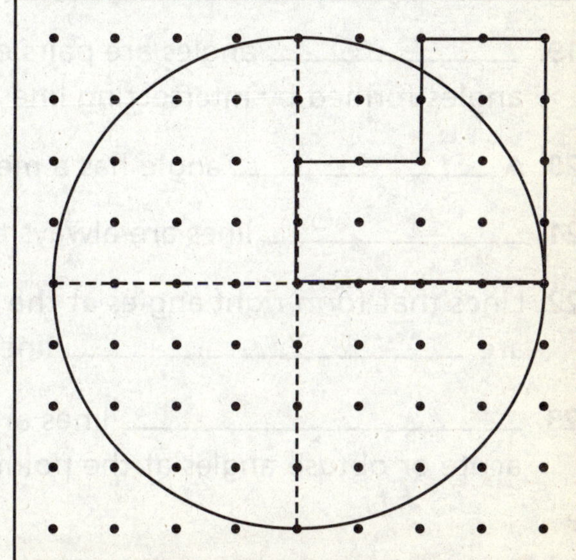

Remembering

Solve.

1. 4.09 + 4.38 = _____

2. 5.6 − 1.8 = _____

3. 16.0 + 2.316 = _____

4. 3.34 + 9.01 = _____

5. 11.70 − 10.358 = _____

6. 8.87 − 4.56 = _____

7. 0.43 + 1.07 = _____

8. 14.4 − 6.2 = _____

9. 14.34 + 11.48 = _____

10. 7.40 + 1.93 = _____

11. 13.4 − 6.28 = _____

12. 8.7 − 4.3 = _____

Solve the Factor Puzzles.

13.

72	
27	15

14.

	6
28	8

15.

8	16
	72

Complete the statements.

16. A _____________ angle has a measure of 180°.

17. A(n) _____________ angle has a measure less than 90°.

18. A(n) _____________ angle has a measure greater than 90° and less than 180°.

19. _____________ angles are pairs of opposite and congruent angles formed by intersecting lines.

20. A _____________ angle has a measure of 90°.

21. _____________ lines are always the same distance apart.

22. Lines that form right angles at the point of intersection are _____________ lines.

23. _____________ lines are lines that form acute or obtuse angles at the point of intersection.

Circles and Angles

Homework

1. In the space below, draw a figure that has at least one line of symmetry.

Consider these letters of the alphabet.

A B C D E F G H I J K L M
N O P Q R S T U V W X Y Z

2. Which letters have line symmetry?

____

____

3. Which letters have rotational symmetry?

____

____

4. Which letters have line symmetry and rotational symmetry?

____

____

Name ___________________ **Date** ___________________

Remembering

Solve for the unknown number.

1. $1.4 + a = 5.7$ _______   2. $e - 1 = 1.75$ _______   3. $b + 0.25 = 1$ _______

4. $2.54 - m = 1.50$ _______   5. $5.6 + c = 6.0$ _______   6. $n - 3.7 = 1.7$ _______

7. $p + 10.01 = 10.45$ _______   8. $3.9 - d = 1.2$ _______   9. $0.5 + s = 0.8$ _______

10. $t - 4.13 = 0.40$ _______   11. $y + 0.8 = 4.1$ _______   12. $5.87 - h = 4.33$ _______

13. $7.4 + r = 9.5$ _______   14. $f - 9.7 = 4.3$ _______   15. $x + 1.88 = 4.91$ _______

16. $8.69 - g = 5.82$ _______   17. $10.04 + k = 11.00$ _______   18. $w - 5.0 = 11.73$ _______

19. What is the measure of the base of a triangle that has a height of 8 centimeters and an area of 24 square centimeters? Explain your thinking.

____

____

____

20. What is the measure of the length of a rectangle that has a width of 2 meters and a perimeter of 14 meters? Explain your thinking.

____

____

____

Round each decimal to the nearest whole number.

21. 12.3 _______   22. 25.6 _______   23. 19.8 _______

24. 10.45 _______   25. 99.9 _______   26. 100.09 _______

27. 41.67 _______   28. 35.70 _______   29. 50.51 _______

   Symmetry

Name _______________ **Date** _______________

Homework

Use the circle graph to answer questions 1–3.

1. Which types of days occur equally often, according to the graph?

   ____

2. If you visited Honolulu for ten days, how many of those days would you expect it to be partly cloudy? Explain your reasoning.

   ____

   ____

   ____

   ____

3. Out of the 365 days in a year, about how many sunny days would you expect in Honolulu? How do you know?

   ____

   ____

   ____

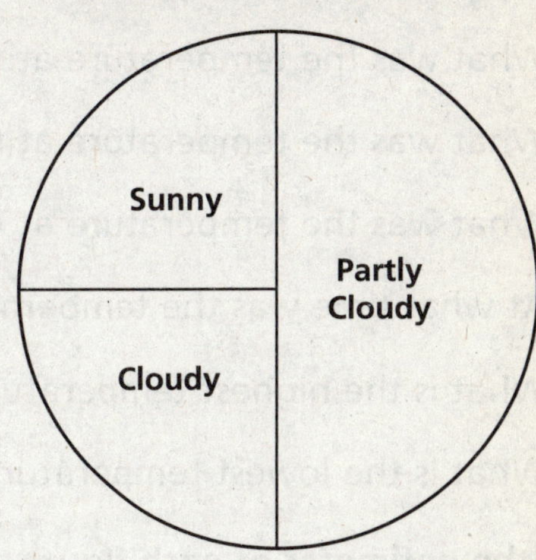

4. Last night, Sharise studied for 60 minutes. The table below shows the subjects she studied and how long she studied each subject. Show the data on this circle graph.

Time Spent Studying	
Subject	**Time**
Science	20 minutes
Reading	30 minutes
Spelling	10 minutes

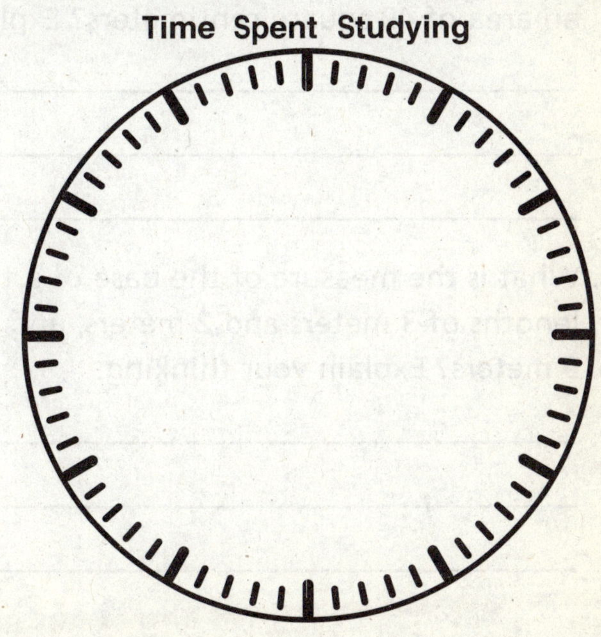

Name   **Date**

Remembering

Use the line graph to answer each question.

1. What was the temperature at 10:00 A.M.? _______

2. What was the temperature at noon? _______

3. What was the temperature at 4:00 P.M.? _______

4. At what time was the temperature 18°C? _______

5. What is the highest temperature? _______

6. What is the lowest temperature? _______

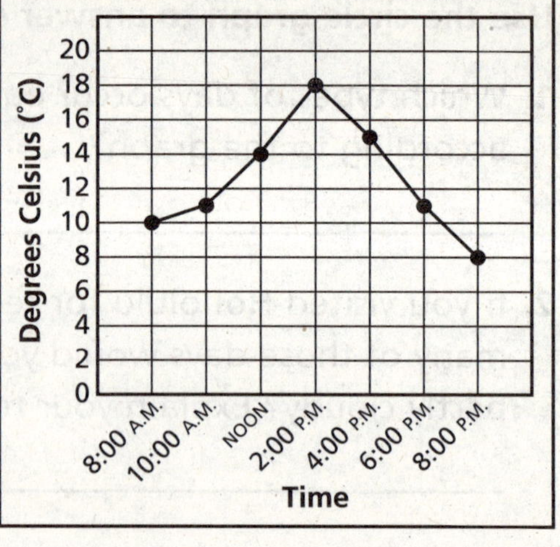

Find the perimeter of each figure.

7.

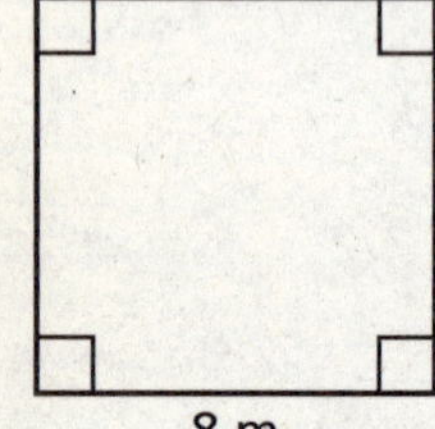

8.

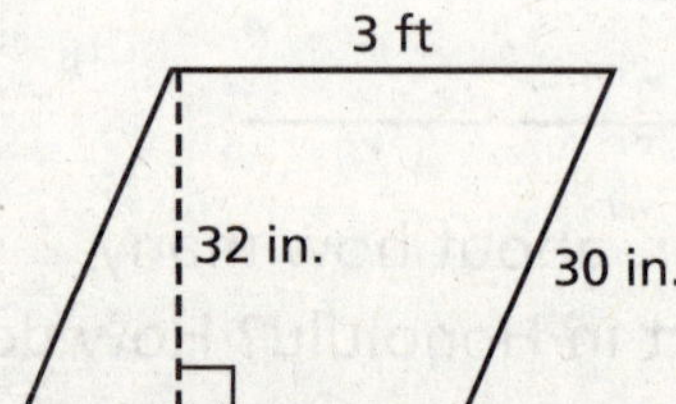

9.

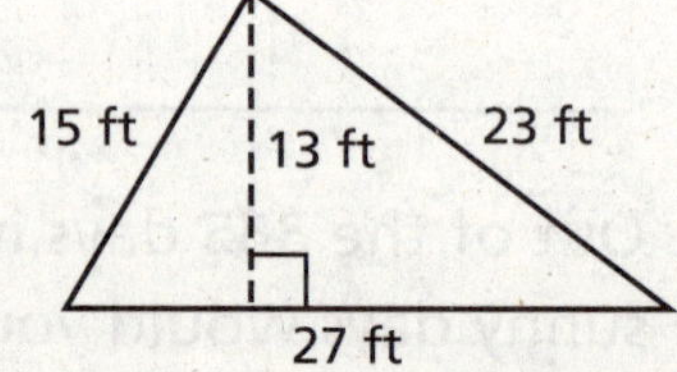

10. What is the measure of the side length of a square that has an area of 49 square centimeters? Explain your thinking.

____

____

____

11. What is the measure of the base of a triangle that has side lengths of 3 meters and 2 meters, and a perimeter of 9 meters? Explain your thinking.

____

____

Homework

Use the given measures to estimate the circumference of each circle. Use 3 for π.

1.

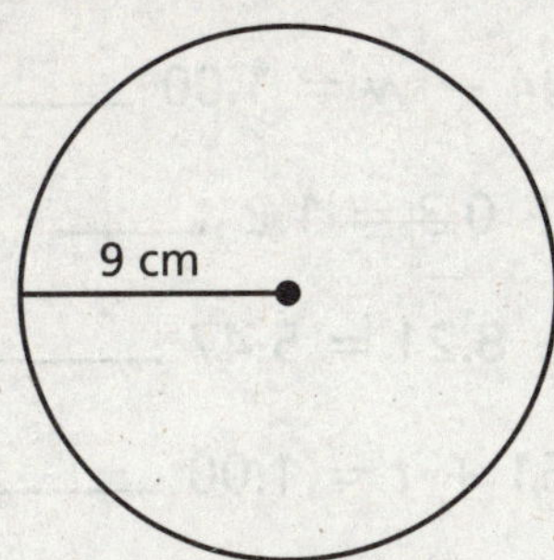

____

2.

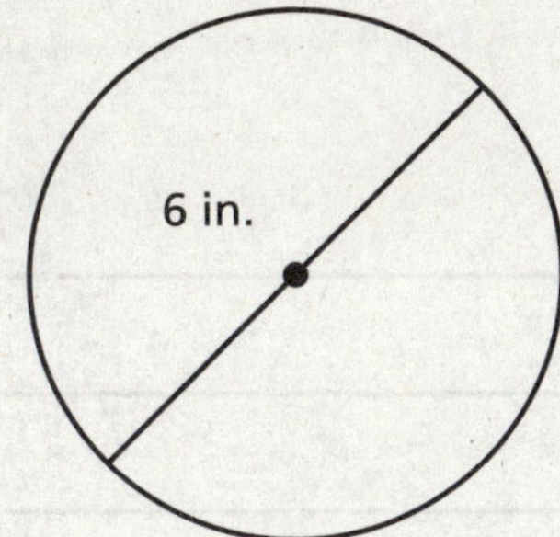

____

3.

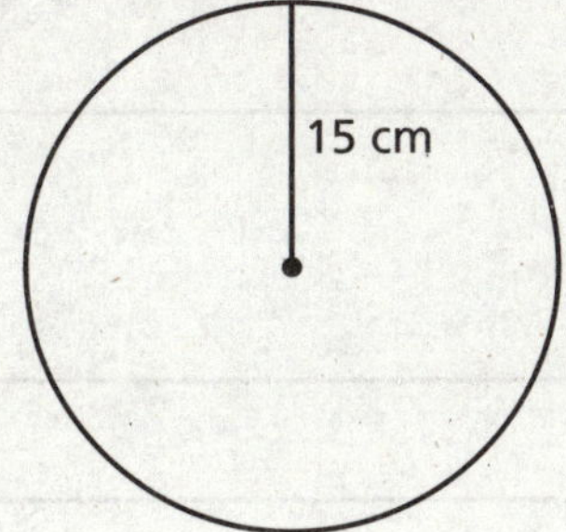

____

4. The circumference of a circle is 24 meters. About how long is a diameter of that circle?

____

5. The circumference of a circle is 30 inches. About how long is a radius of that circle?

____

Name _______________ **Date** _______________

Remembering

Solve for the unknown.

1. $z + 0.02 = 0.94$ _____   **2.** $12.4 - b = 8.5$ _____   **3.** $3.46 + d = 4.10$ _____

4. $p - 8.0 = 4.9$ _____   **5.** $m + 0.57 = 0.61$ _____   **6.** $2.44 - w = 1.00$ _____

7. $14.1 + e = 16.0$ _____   **8.** $n - 3.00 = 7.29$ _____   **9.** $a + 0.3 = 1.2$ _____

10. $8.56 - h = 2.50$ _____   **11.** $4.4 + h = 5.5$ _____   **12.** $s - 8.21 = 5.47$ _____

13. $r + 14.1 = 18.7$ _____   **14.** $7.8 - x = 6.9$ _____   **15.** $0.51 + t = 1.00$ _____

16. $y - 0.4 = 0.1$ _____   **17.** $c + 7.16 = 9.01$ _____   **18.** $1.32 - f = 0.74$ _____

Find the area of each shaded region. Explain your thinking.

19.

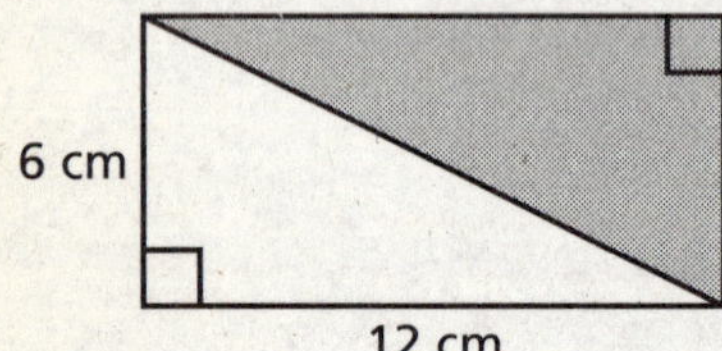

____

____

____

____

____

20.

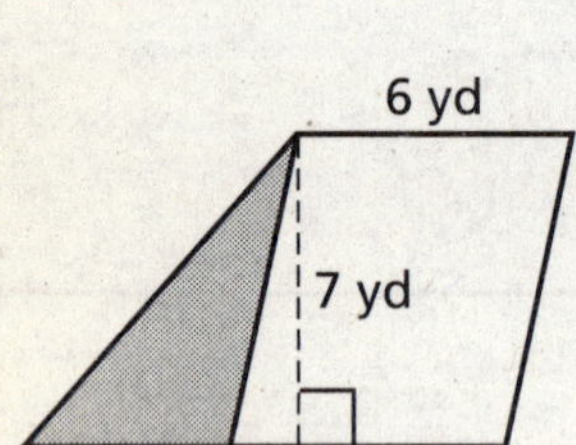

____

____

____

____

____

21.

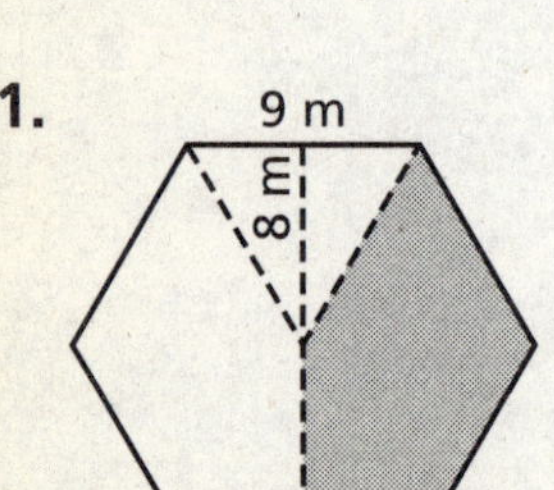

____

____

____

____

____

Homework

Circle the greater fraction. Then write the correct sign (> or <) between them.

1. $\frac{1}{3}$ $\frac{1}{4}$ 2. $\frac{1}{9}$ $\frac{1}{7}$ 3. $\frac{1}{98}$ $\frac{1}{99}$

4. $\frac{5}{7}$ 1   5. 1 $\frac{7}{8}$ 6. 1 $\frac{51}{52}$

7. $\frac{5}{6}$ $\frac{4}{6}$ 8. $\frac{51}{68}$ $\frac{53}{68}$ 9. $\frac{2}{5}$ $\frac{2}{8}$

10. $\frac{1}{10}$ $\frac{1}{2}$ 11. $\frac{9}{10}$ $\frac{9}{100}$ 12. $\frac{3}{5}$ $\frac{3}{4}$

Show your work.

13. Claire and Ramona each have a banana the same size. Claire cuts hers into fourths. Ramona cuts hers into sixths. Whose banana has bigger pieces?

____

14. Jorge rode his bicycle $\frac{2}{5}$ of a mile. Andrew rode his $\frac{4}{5}$ of a mile. Julio rode his $\frac{3}{5}$ of a mile. Who rode the farthest?

____

15. At a basketball game, Tessa scored $\frac{1}{10}$ of the points, Erica scored $\frac{1}{12}$ of the points, and Kenya scored $\frac{1}{9}$ of the points. Who scored the most points?

____

16. Tony and Kurt are reading the same book. Tony has read $\frac{136}{200}$ of the book. Kurt has read $\frac{124}{200}$ of the book. Who has read more of it?

____

Remembering

Solve the Factor Puzzles.

1.
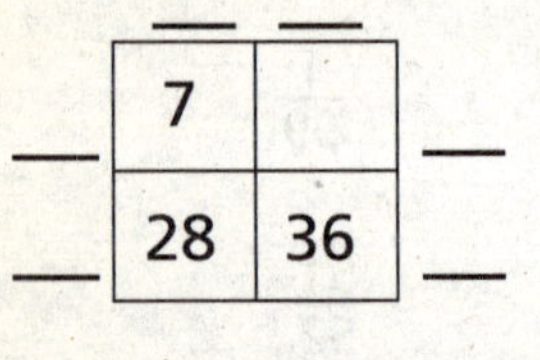

2.

	5
16	8

3.

40	56
	35

4.

12	14
60	

5.

3	
18	24

6.

	21
20	35

7.

16	32
	24

8.

40	55
32	

Find the perimeter and area.

9.
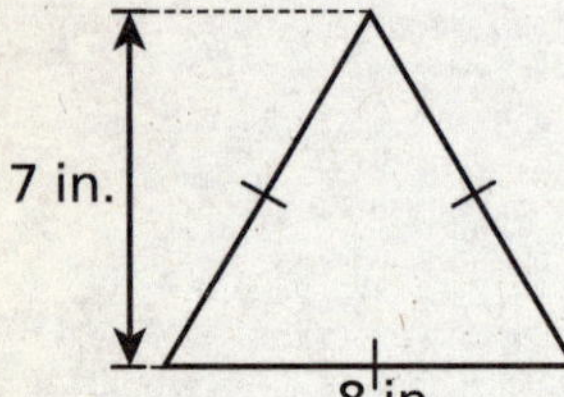

7 in.

8 in.

P = ______________

A = ______________

10.
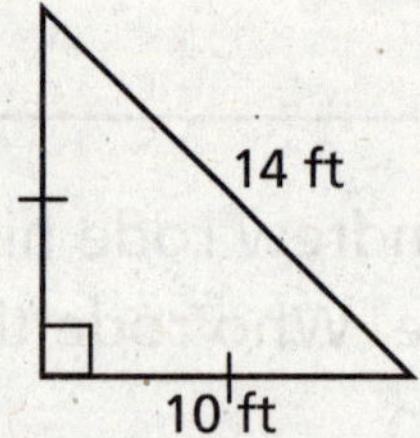

14 ft

10 ft

P = ______________

A = ______________

11.
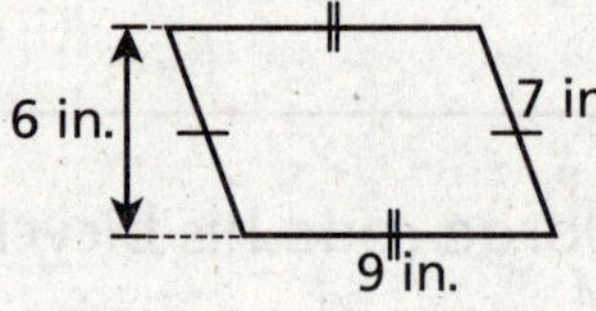

6 in.   7 in.

9 in.

P = ______________

A = ______________

Solve.   *Show your work.*

12. At your lemonade stand you charge $0.50 for a half cup and $0.75 for a full cup. At the end of the day, you see that 12 cups have been used and you have made $8.00. How many of each size of drink did you sell?

____

13. Anna is 3 years older than Laura. The product of their ages is double the sum of their ages. How old are they?

____

____

Name _______________________ **Date** _______________

Homework

Add or subtract.

1. $\frac{1}{6} + \frac{4}{6} =$ _______   **2.** $\frac{3}{7} + \frac{2}{7} + \frac{1}{7} =$ _______   **3.** $\frac{3}{5} - \frac{1}{5} =$ _______

Find *n* or *d*.

4. $\frac{7}{8} - \frac{2}{8} = \frac{n}{8}$ **5.** $\frac{3}{4} - \frac{1}{4} = \frac{2}{d}$

   $n =$ _______ $d =$ _______

6. $\frac{4}{15} + \frac{6}{15} + \frac{2}{15} = \frac{n}{15}$ **7.** $\frac{2}{d} + \frac{2}{d} + \frac{2}{d} + \frac{2}{d} = \frac{8}{15}$

   $n =$ _______ $d =$ _______

8. $\frac{5}{12} + \frac{2}{12} + \frac{3}{12} = \frac{10}{d}$ **9.** $\frac{1}{d} + \frac{1}{d} + \frac{1}{d} + \frac{1}{d} + \frac{1}{d} = \frac{d}{d}$

   $d =$ _______ $d =$ _______

Circle the greater fraction.

10. $\frac{1}{5}$ $\frac{1}{9}$ **11.** $\frac{3}{d}$ $\frac{7}{d}$ **12.** $\frac{8}{d}$ $\frac{6}{d}$

13. What is $\frac{n}{d}$? _______________

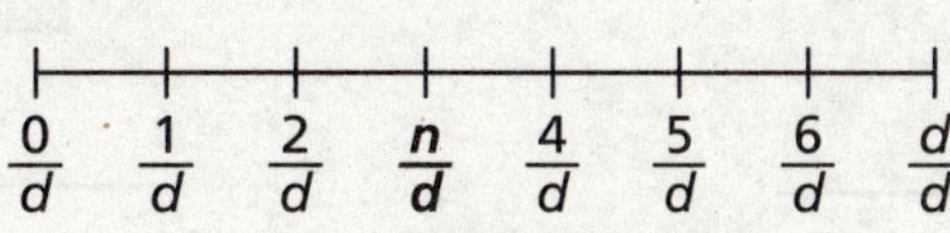

14. What fraction is circled? _______________

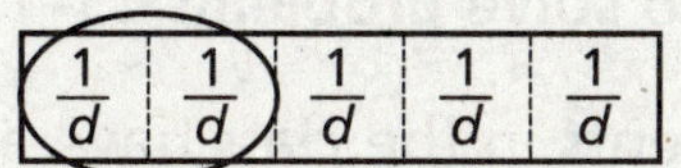

15. What fraction of the class likes winter or summer best? _______________

16. What fraction of the class likes fall best? _______________

17. Use the circle graph to find *d*.

   $\frac{3}{4} + \frac{2}{d} = 1$ $d =$ _______________

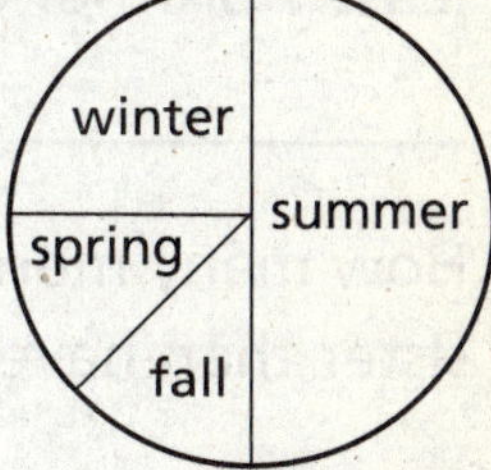

18. The grade 5 class sold cheese for a fundraiser. What fraction of the orders did each of the four students take?

____

____

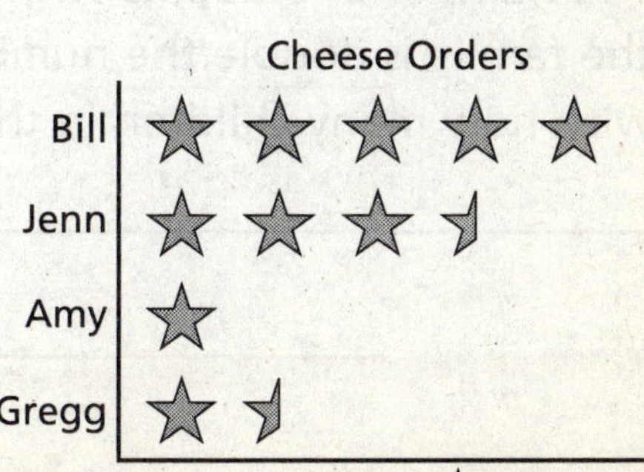

Remembering

Add or subtract.

1. $0.75 + 0.2 =$ _______   **2.** $3.5 + 2.5 =$ _______   **3.** $0.5 - 0.2 =$ _______

4. $0.175 + 0.250 =$ _______   **5.** $5.835 + 1.35 =$ _______   **6.** $3.7 - 1.6 =$ _______

7. $0.072 - 0.03 =$ _______   **8.** $0.001 + 0.959 =$ _______   **9.** $8.206 + 1.5 =$ _______

10. $3.504 - 1.25 =$ _______   **11.** $4.0 - 0.8 =$ _______   **12.** $6.34 - 2.28 =$ _______

Find the area of the shaded region.

13.

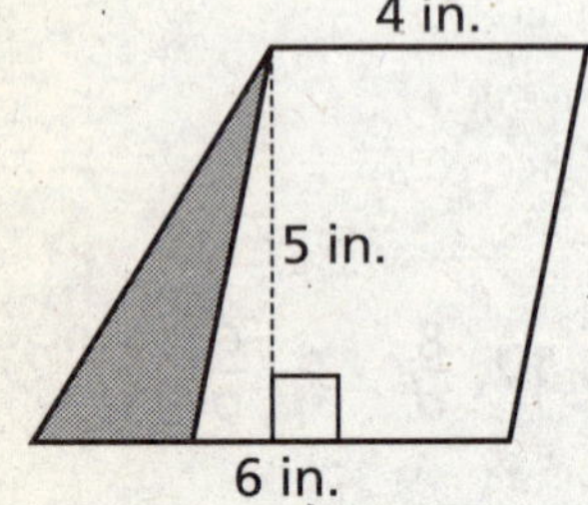

____

14.

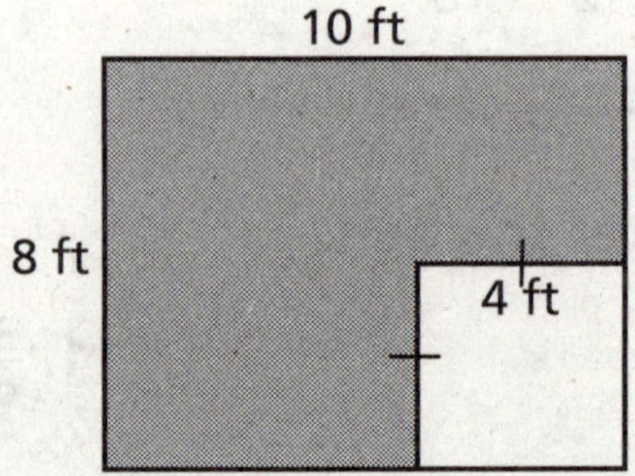

____

Use the bar graph to solve problems 15–17.

15. How many students in the class have at least 1 brother or sister?

____

16. How many more students have 1 brother or sister than have 3?

____

17. The number of students with 2 children in the family is double the number of students with how many children in the family?

____

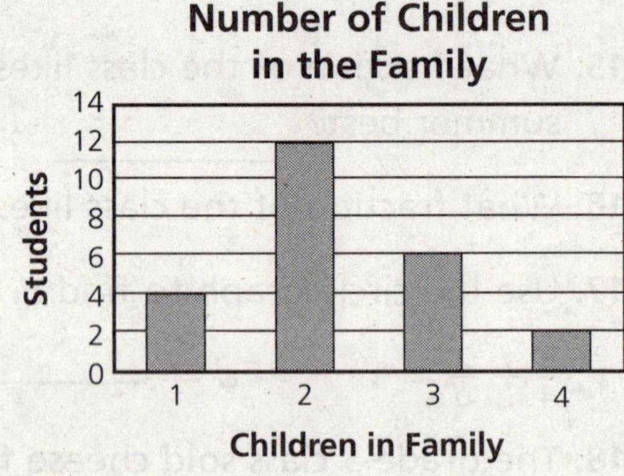

Name ___________________________ **Date** ___________________

Homework

Add or subtract.

1. $\frac{4}{7} - \frac{1}{7} =$ _______

2. $\frac{6}{52} + \frac{4}{52} =$ _______

3. $\frac{8}{15} + \frac{7}{15} =$ _______

4. $\frac{5}{60} + \frac{12}{60} =$ _______

5. $\frac{6}{37} + \frac{6}{37} =$ _______

6. $\frac{50}{100} - \frac{40}{100} =$ _______

Find *n* or *d*.

7. $1 - \frac{7}{13} = \frac{n}{d}$

$\frac{n}{d} =$ _______

8. $1 - \frac{5}{40} = \frac{n}{d}$

$\frac{n}{d} =$ _______

9. $\frac{5}{8} + \frac{n}{d} = 1$

$\frac{n}{d} =$ _______

10. $\frac{3}{16} + \frac{n}{d} = 1$

$\frac{n}{d} =$ _______

11. $\frac{20}{25} + \frac{n}{d} = 1$

$\frac{n}{d} =$ _______

12. $\frac{150}{200} + \frac{n}{d} = 1$

$\frac{n}{d} =$ _______

Solve.

13. Hannah's joke made $\frac{25}{32}$ of the class laugh. What fraction of the class did not laugh at her joke?

____

14. Tyler's joke made $\frac{28}{32}$ of the class laugh. What fraction of the class did not laugh at his joke?

____

15. Who told the funnier joke?

____

16. In Mrs. Lopez' class, $\frac{9}{24}$ of the students take the bus to school and $\frac{8}{24}$ come in a car. The rest of the students walk to school. What fraction of the students walk?

____

Remembering

Find the unknown.

1. $6b = 42$

$b =$ _______

2. $5c + 1 = 36$

$c =$ _______

3. $d = (4 \times 5) + (2 \times 9)$

$d =$ _______

4. $64 \div s = 8$

$s =$ _______

5. $\frac{1}{6}m = 9$

$m =$ _______

6. $28 + p = 32$

$p =$ _______

7. $7(5 + 3) = t$

$t =$ _______

8. $k = 4(6 + 3)$

$k =$ _______

9. $6v = 72$

$v =$ _______

Label each angle as acute, obtuse, or right.

10. 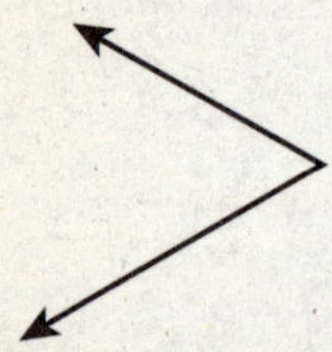   **11.** 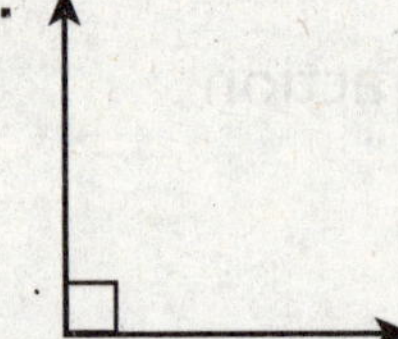   **12.** 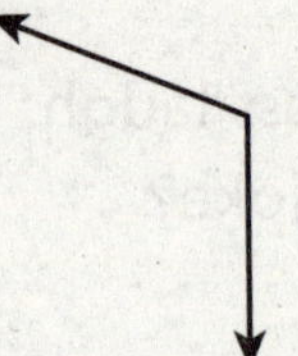   **13.** 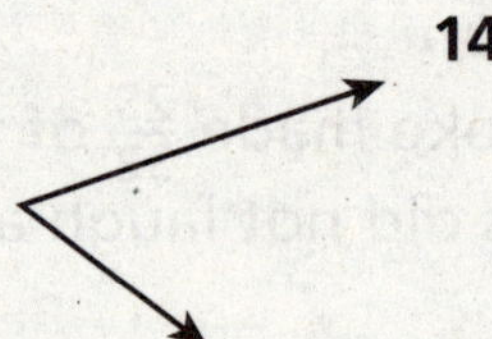   **14.** 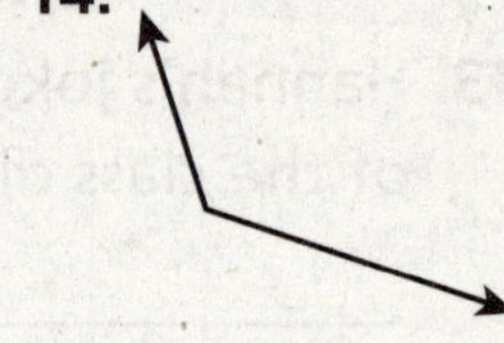

_______   _______   _______   _______   _______

Solve.

15. The bookstore staff sold 700 books in one week. If they sold the same number of books each day, how many books had they sold after 3 days?

____

16. The grade 5 students are raising money for a trip that will cost $175. Students have taken orders for 92 buckets of frozen cookie dough at a price of $6.00 each. If the students have to pay $4.00 for each bucket, will they make enough money for their trip?

____

Name _______________________ **Date** _______________________

Homework

What fraction of each group of ice cream cones has a cherry?

1.  _______________

2.  _______________

3.  _______________

4. Answer the Puzzled Penguin's letter.

Dear Math Student,

I just learned that $\frac{1}{3}$ of the students in my class play soccer. My friend in another class says that $\frac{1}{3}$ of the students in her class also play soccer. I said, "Oh, then the same number of students play soccer in each class." She answered, "No, I don't think that's true."

Now I'm confused. If the same **fraction** of students play soccer, wouldn't that mean that the same **number** of students play soccer? Who do you think is right? Can you explain this to me?

Thank you.

Puzzled Penguin

____

____

____

____

____

____

____

____

____

Remembering

1. $692 + 463 =$ _______

2. $1,843 + 199 =$ _______

3. $567 + 4,968 =$ _______

4. $746 - 99 =$ _______

5. $2,420 - 398 =$ _______

6. $62,685 - 810 =$ _______

7. $6,874 + 552 =$ _______

8. $7,502 + 2,539 =$ _______

9. $29,463 + 14,054 =$ _______

10. $3,985 - 1,775 =$ _______

Find the perimeter and area of each figure.

11.

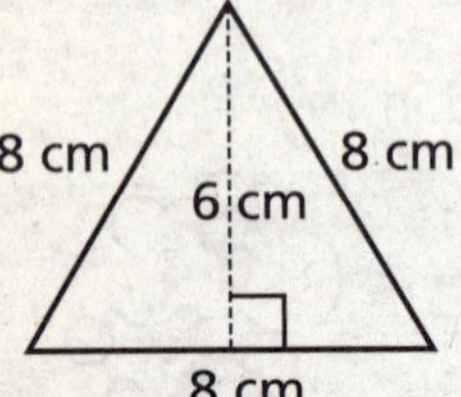

$P =$ _______

$A =$ _______

12.

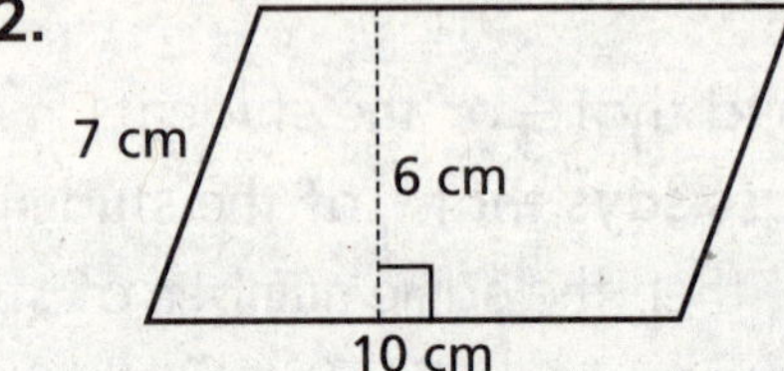

$P =$ _______

$A =$ _______

13.

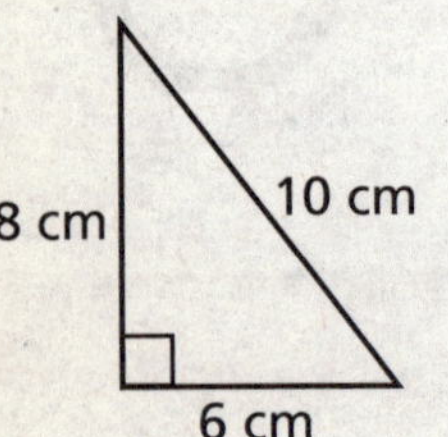

$P =$ _______

$A =$ _______

14.

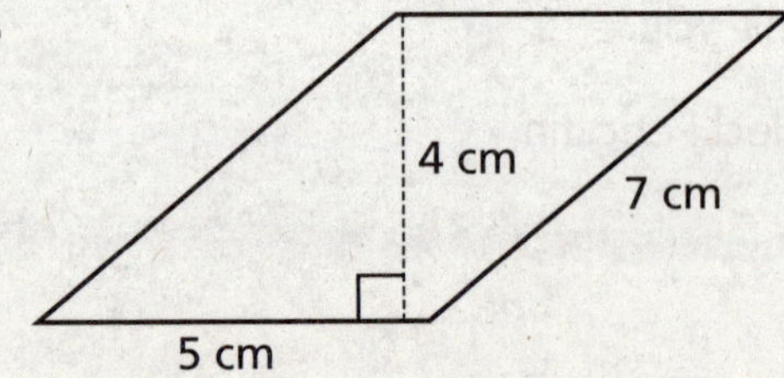

$P =$ _______

$A =$ _______

Solve.

15. Hayley has twice as many stamps in her collection as Kevin does. Kevin has three times as many stamps as Jen. If Kevin has 60 stamps, how many do the three friends have altogether?

____

16. Jon has 32 books on his shelf. He has 7 times the number of mystery books as science fiction. How many of each kind does he have?

____

    Relate Fractions and Wholes

Homework

Name the mixed number shown by the shaded parts.

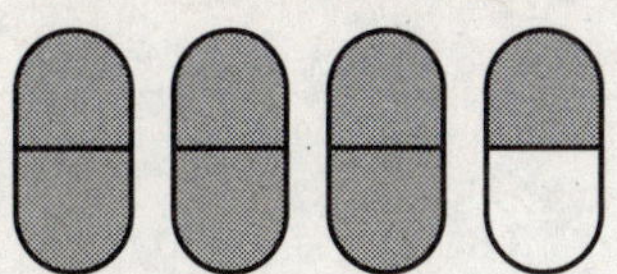   

1. _____________ 2. _____________ 3. _____________

Write the mixed number as an improper fraction.

4. $2\frac{1}{3} =$ _______ 5. $4\frac{2}{5} =$ _______ 6. $3\frac{3}{4} =$ _______ 7. $1\frac{5}{8} =$ _______

Write the improper fraction as a mixed number.

8. $\frac{7}{6} =$ _______ 9. $\frac{8}{3} =$ _______ 10. $\frac{9}{2} =$ _______ 11. $\frac{10}{7} =$ _______

Complete. Give the answer as a mixed number.

12. $\frac{3}{5} + \frac{4}{5} =$ _______ 13. $\frac{6}{4} + \frac{3}{4} =$ _______

14. $\frac{2}{9} + \frac{8}{9} =$ _______ 15. $7 + \frac{2}{3} =$ _______

Solve.

Show your work.

16. Alicia walked $\frac{7}{8}$ mile on Saturday and $\frac{6}{8}$ mile on Sunday. How far did she walk over the weekend? Give the answer as a mixed number.

____

17. The dark chain is $\frac{5}{12}$ yard long. The white one is $\frac{9}{12}$ yard long. How long will they be if they are joined? Give the answer as a mixed number.

____

Remembering

Solve.

1. The dog has gone $\frac{5}{8}$ of the way across the yard. How much farther does it have to go to reach the gate? __________

2. The cat has gone $\frac{7}{16}$ of the way across the yard. How much farther does it have to go to reach the gate? __________

3. I cleaned $\frac{6}{9}$ of my room, and my friend cleaned $\frac{2}{9}$ of my room. How much of my room do we still have to clean? __________

4. Mrs. Spencer's class is signing up to play sports. $\frac{8}{26}$ of the students want to play soccer and $\frac{12}{26}$ want to play basketball. The rest of the students want to play baseball. What fraction of the students wants to play baseball? __________

Solve the Factor Puzzles.

5.

5	
25	35

6.

	6
12	8

7.

30	27
	18

8.

	64
36	72

9.

9	12
21	

10.

4	
10	25

Homework

Complete each equation. Express answers as mixed numbers.

1. $\frac{3}{5} + \frac{4}{5} =$ _____

2. $\frac{6}{4} + \frac{3}{4} =$ _____

3. $4\frac{2}{9} + 2\frac{7}{9} =$ _____

4. $1\frac{7}{8} + 3\frac{3}{8} =$ _____

5. $4\frac{1}{2} + 5\frac{1}{2} =$ _____

6. $3\frac{1}{7} + 2\frac{1}{7} =$ _____

7. $1\frac{5}{7} + 1\frac{3}{7} =$ _____

8. $50\frac{1}{3} + 50\frac{1}{3} =$ _____

9. A group of campers hiked for $5\frac{3}{4}$ hours today and $6\frac{3}{4}$ hours yesterday. How many hours did they hike in all? _____________

10. What fractional parts are shown on the number line below? _____________

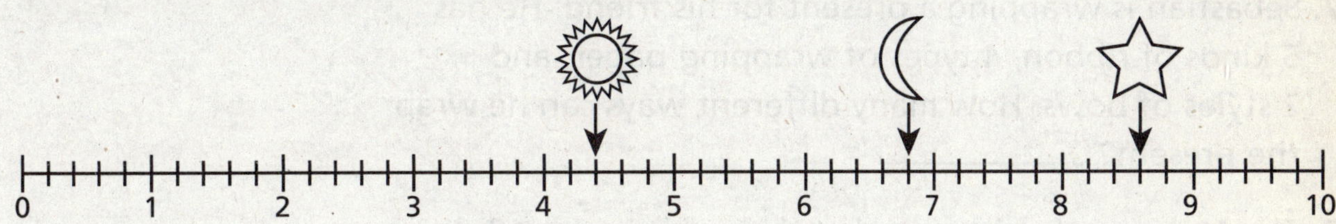

11. What mixed number is marked by the sun? _____________

12. What mixed number is marked by the moon? _____________

13. What mixed number is marked by the star? _____________

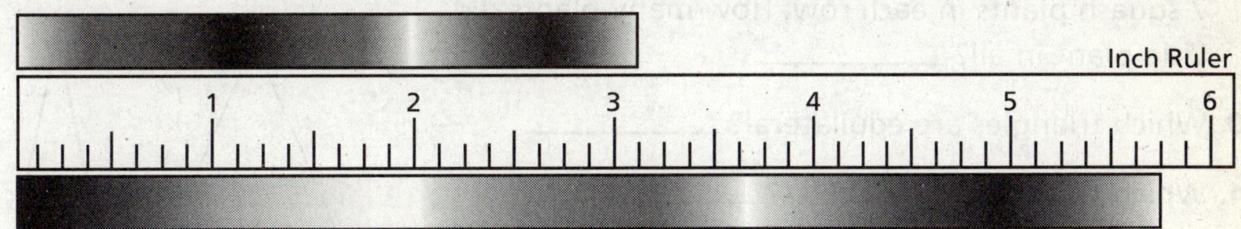

14. What fractional parts are shown on the inch ruler above? _____________

15. How long is the ribbon on top? _____________

16. How long is the ribbon on the bottom? _____________

17. If you place the two ribbons end-to-end, how long are they? _____________

   Add Fractions Greater Than One **117**

Name **Date**

Remembering

Add.

1.	363.12	2.	86,435.717	3.	1,382,104.4050
	+ 422.51		+ 3,385.122		+ 34,208,010.6334

Subtract.

4.	945.3	5.	12,532.36	6.	9,112,001.880
	− 412.1		− 10,801.45		− 8,750,500.224

Solve.

Show your work.

7. Sebastián is wrapping a present for his friend. He has 5 kinds of ribbon, 4 types of wrapping paper, and 2 styles of bows. How many different ways can he wrap the present? _____________

8. The Mahoney family stayed at the seashore for 18 days. They stayed 3 times as long as the Adorno family. How long did the Adorno family stay? _____________

9. Lisle planted 4 rows of tomatoes with 6 tomato plants in each row. He also planted 3 rows of squash with 7 squash plants in each row. How many plants did Lisle plant in all? _____________

10. Which triangles are equilateral? _____________

11. Which triangles are isosceles? _____________

12. Which triangles are scalene? _____________

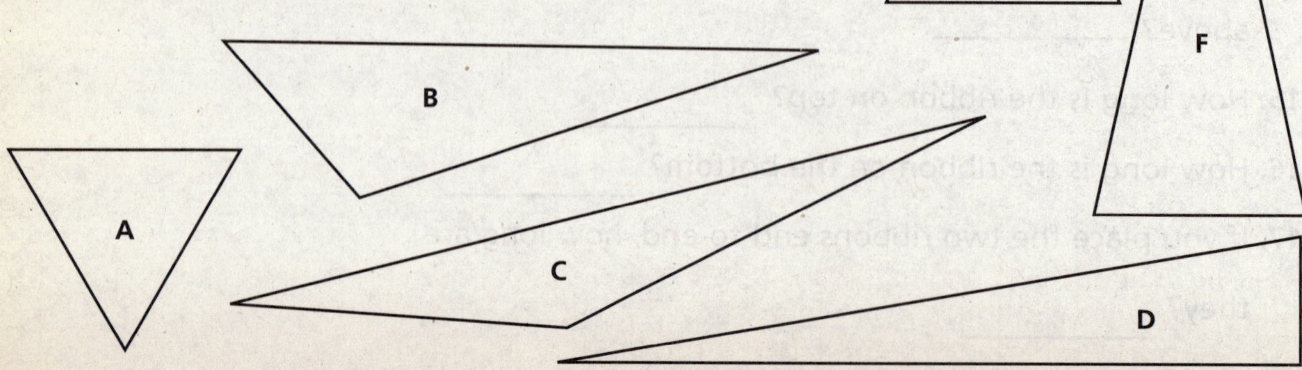

Add Fractions Greater Than One

Homework

Name _______________________ **Date** _______________________

Subtract.

1. $1\frac{7}{9} - \frac{4}{9} =$ _____ **2.** $4\frac{6}{7} - 2\frac{5}{7} =$ _____ **3.** $6\frac{4}{5} - 3\frac{2}{5} =$ _____ **4.** $25\frac{5}{8} - 10\frac{1}{8} =$ _____

5. $2 - \frac{1}{3} =$ _____ **6.** $5\frac{3}{8} - 2\frac{7}{8} =$ _____ **7.** $2\frac{1}{6} - 1\frac{5}{6} =$ _____ **8.** $7\frac{2}{5} - 3\frac{3}{5} =$ _____

Solve. *Show your work.*

9. I made a clay snake $9\frac{5}{8}$ inches long, but a section $1\frac{7}{8}$ inches long broke off. How long is the snake now?

____

10. Deacon had $12\frac{1}{3}$ ounces of juice, but he drank $3\frac{2}{3}$ ounces. How much juice is left?

____

How long will each log be after a piece is cut off? Check your answer by adding the lengths of the two pieces.

11. cut off $3\frac{2}{6}$ feet | $10\frac{5}{6}$ feet total

_____ feet left

12. cut off $4\frac{3}{4}$ feet | $7\frac{1}{4}$ feet total

_____ feet left

13. cut off $6\frac{2}{9}$ feet | $11\frac{4}{9}$ feet total

_____ feet left

14. cut off $3\frac{2}{5}$ feet | $6\frac{2}{5}$ feet total

_____ feet left

Name _______________________ **Date** _______________________

Remembering

Write > or < to show which is greater.

1. 209 _______ 290

2. 30,502 _______ 30,052

3. 128,779 _______ 127,999

4. 360.099 _______ 306.990

5. 41,772.012 _______ 41,770.228

6. 100.096 _______ 100.10

Solve. Use multiplication or division.

Show your work.

7. Jenny prepared 4 rows for bean plants. She can fit 16 bean plants in each row. How many bean plants can she grow?

____

8. A school bus can carry 60 students. How many buses should a school order to take 520 students on a trip?

____

9. A hummingbird's heart beats about 4 times in one second while it is resting. At this rate, how many times does its heart beat in one hour? in one day?

____

Label each triangle acute, right, or obtuse. Briefly explain.

10. 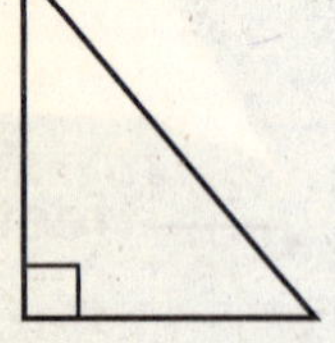

____

____

11. 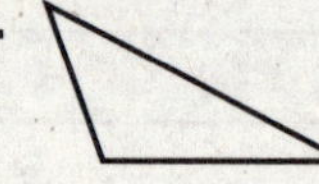

____

____

12. 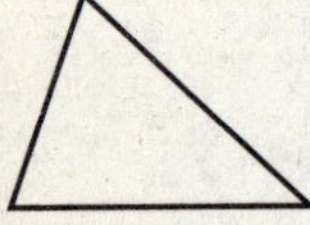

____

____

13. 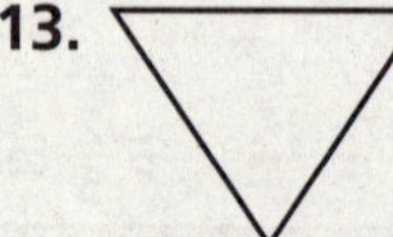

____

____

Subtract Mixed Numbers

Homework

Subtract.

1. $\frac{4}{5} - \frac{1}{5} =$ _____

2. $9\frac{5}{8} - 3\frac{3}{8} =$ _____

3. $5\frac{1}{6} - 2\frac{5}{6} =$ _____

4. $18\frac{4}{9} - 10\frac{5}{9} =$ _____

5. $3 - \frac{1}{4} =$ _____

6. $6\frac{3}{8} - 2\frac{7}{8} =$ _____

7. $2\frac{1}{3} - 1\frac{2}{3} =$ _____

8. $6\frac{5}{7} - 3\frac{3}{7} =$ _____

Solve.

Show your work.

9. Cory planned to practice the piano for $1\frac{1}{4}$ hours but he spent $\frac{3}{4}$ hour playing computer games. How long did he actually practice the piano?

____

10. Hala made $\frac{4}{10}$ of the hits at the baseball game and Ernestina made $\frac{1}{10}$. Who made more hits? How many more?

____

The campers at Tall Pines Camp saw some animal tracks in the woods. They measured them and made a table showing all the different lengths. Use the table to complete exercises 11–15.

Animal Track	Length
Raccoon	$1\frac{2}{8}$ in.
Fox	$3\frac{1}{8}$ in.
Deer	$1\frac{6}{8}$ in.
Moose	$5\frac{7}{8}$ in.

11. Which track is longer, the raccoon track or the fox track? by how much?

____

12. How much shorter is the deer track than the moose track?

____

13. How much longer is the fox track than the deer track?

____

14. How much shorter is the raccoon track than the deer track?

____

15. List the animal tracks in order from the longest to the shortest.

____

Remembering

Find the unknown number in each equation.

1. $s = 4 + (3 \times 9)$ $s =$ _______

2. $12 = t - 7$ $t =$ _______

3. $k = 28 - (2 \times 6)$ $k =$ _______

4. $(14 - 9) \times 3 = m$ $m =$ _______

5. $y = (112 - 94) \times 4$ $y =$ _______

6. $36 = b + 12$ $b =$ _______

7. $h - 15 = 52$ $h =$ _______

8. $70 = p + (3 \times 6)$ $p =$ _______

Solve.

Show your work.

9. Lina has $20 with her. She buys 3 items that cost
   $6.98, $4.49, and $7.75. Can she also buy a bottle of
   juice for $1.29?

   ____

10. Asim is 11 years old. He went on the bus with his mom,
    his aunt, his two younger brothers, and his aunt's
    7-year-old daughter. Tickets cost $1.60 for an adult and
    $0.80 for a child. How much did the trip cost?

    ____

11. Graph the data in the table on the circle below.
    Don't forget to label the graph.

Favorite Fruit	
Fruit	**Number**
Orange	16
Banana	2
Apple	4
Grape	8
Other	6

     Comparison Situations

Name _______________ **Date** _______________

Homework

The workers at Willow Green Animal Shelter recently took in four new animals. They decided to measure each animal and record the measurements in a table. Use this table to complete exercises 1–4.

Animal	Length
Duck	$1\frac{5}{12}$ ft
Cat	$2\frac{8}{12}$ ft
Dog	$3\frac{10}{12}$ ft
Pig	$3\frac{4}{12}$ ft

1. Which is longer, the pig or the dog? how much longer?

____

2. How much shorter is the duck than the cat?

____

3. How much longer is the dog than the duck?

____

4. How much shorter is the cat than the pig?

____

Troy and Francisco decided to make gingerbread people using this recipe. Use it to complete exercises 5–9.

Gingerbread People
$\frac{1}{4}$ pound butter
1 cup sugar
$\frac{1}{4}$ teaspoon salt
$2\frac{1}{4}$ cups flour
1 cup molasses
$1\frac{3}{4}$ teaspoons soda
$2\frac{1}{4}$ teaspoons ginger
2 eggs

5. Troy has $\frac{3}{4}$ cup of sugar and Francisco has $\frac{2}{4}$ cup. How much sugar do they have in all?

____

6. Will they have any sugar left after making the cookies? How much?

____

7. Troy and Francisco have $\frac{3}{4}$ cups of flour. How much more do they need?

____

8. At the party, the girls ate $\frac{5}{8}$ of the cookies and the boys ate $\frac{3}{8}$. How many cookies are left?

____

9. Troy and Francisco started with 1 pound of butter. How much do they have now?

____

  Mixed Practice with Like Fractions **123**

Name ___________________   **Date** ___________________

Remembering

Circle the greater fraction in each pair. Write a greater than (>) or less than (<) sign between them.

1. $\frac{6}{700}$ ◯ $\frac{4}{700}$

2. $3\frac{4}{8}$ ◯ $3\frac{7}{8}$

3. $7\frac{9}{10}$ ◯ $7\frac{5}{10}$

4. $10\frac{1}{4}$ ◯ $9\frac{8}{4}$

Find each unknown number.

5. $7a = 56$ $a =$ ______

6. $9 \times d = 81$ $d =$ ______

7. $42 \times 0 = m$ $m =$ ______

8. $27 \div 3 = a$ $a =$ ______

9. $36 \div 12 = q$ $q =$ ______

10. $n \times 5 = 75$ $n =$ ______

11. $y \times 4 = 48$ $y =$ ______

12. $72 = 8h$ $h =$ ______

Find the perimeter of each figure.

Show your work.

13.

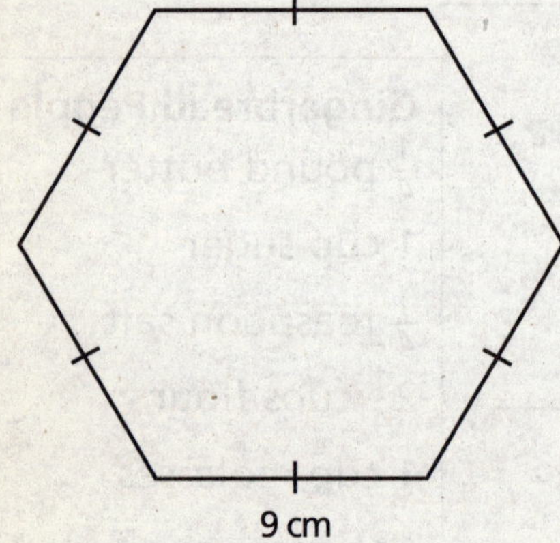

9 cm

Perimeter = ______

14.

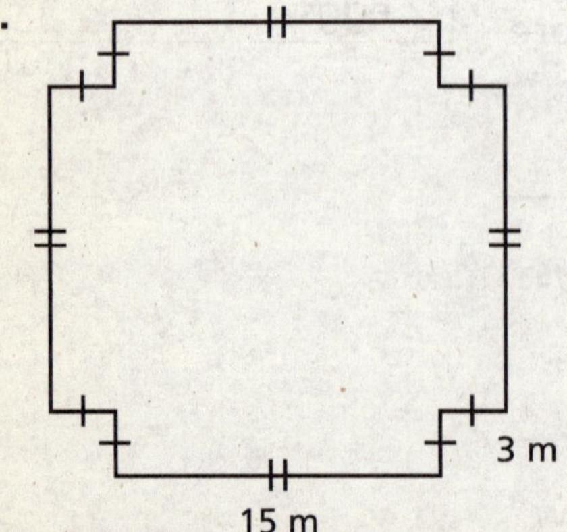

3 m

15 m

Perimeter = ______

          Mixed Practice with Like Fractions

Homework

1. Write a chain of equivalent fractions for the shaded parts.

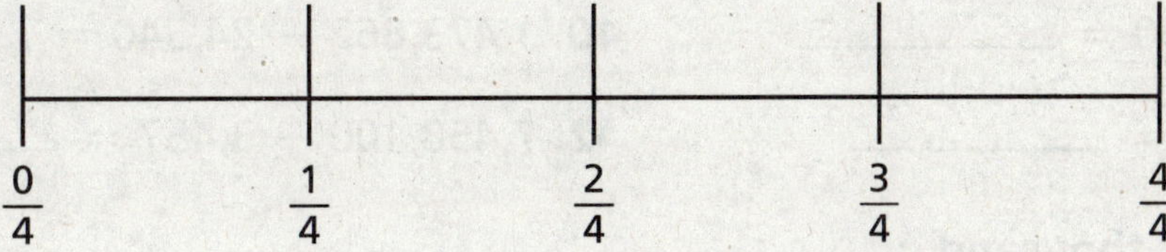

________ = ________ = ________ = ________ = ________

Use the number lines to complete exercises 2–7.

Fourths

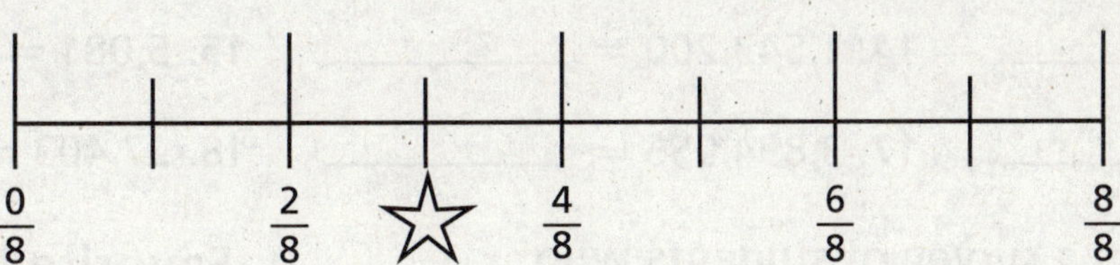

Eighths

Twelfths

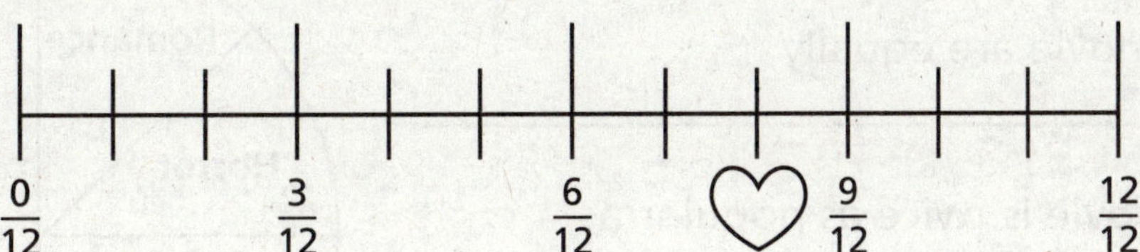

2. What fraction is marked by the star? __________

3. What fraction is marked by the heart? __________

4. If you have $\frac{3}{4}$ cup of flour, how many eighths do

you have? __________

5. If you have $\frac{3}{12}$ of an orange, how many fourths do

you have? __________

6. Which is larger, $\frac{3}{4}$ or $\frac{10}{12}$? __________

7. Give two equivalent fractions for $\frac{6}{8}$. __________

　　　　Discover Equivalent Fractions **125**

Remembering

Add.

1. 4,560 + 52,973 = _______________

2. 581,002 + 26,596 = _______________

3. 4,300,129 + 3,426 = _______________

4. 321,589 + 1,000,000 = _______________

5. 8,601,308 + 585,434 = _______________

6. 2,474,767 + 5,687,136 = _______________

Subtract.

7. 398,000 − 213,546 = _______________

8. 5,439,456 − 1,217,388 = _______________

9. 984,305 − 411,900 = _______________

10. 1,473,862 − 24,540 = _______________

11. 846,549 − 2,308 = _______________

12. 7,458,100 − 3,457 = _______________

Round to the nearest thousand.

13. 14,541 = _______________

14. 1,543,200 = _______________

15. 5,081 = _______________

16. 800,760 = _______________

17. 3,894,956 = _______________

18. 27,403 = _______________

This graph represents a survey of students who were asked to name their favorite type of movie.

19. Which types of movie are equally popular? _______________

20. Which type of movie is twice as popular as romance movies? _______________

21. If 50 students named action as their favorite type of movie, how many students named horror as their favorite? _______________

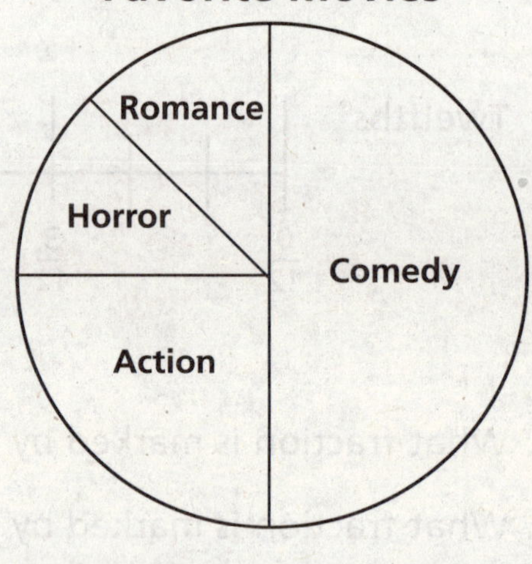

Show your work.

Solve.

22. The Carsons drove 654 km on Monday, 792 km on Tuesday, and 517 km on Wednesday. How many kilometers did they drive in total over the 3 days?

____

23. Otis is 3,750 days old and Casey is 4,539 days old. How many days older than Otis is Casey?

____

   Discover Equivalent Fractions

Homework

1. Write a chain of equivalent fractions for the shaded parts.

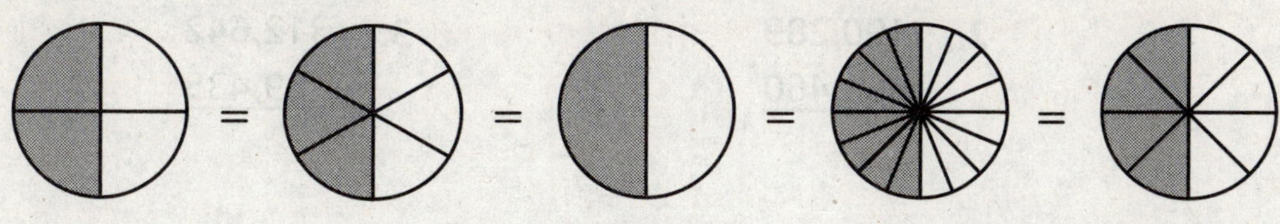

________ = ________ = ________ = ________ = ________

Write the multiplier or divisor for each pair of equivalent fractions.

2. $\frac{4}{12} = \frac{1}{3}$

Divisor = ________

3. $\frac{2}{9} = \frac{6}{27}$

Multiplier = ________

4. $\frac{6}{60} = \frac{1}{10}$

Divisor = ________

5. $\frac{3}{10} = \frac{15}{50}$

Multiplier = ________

6. $\frac{21}{56} = \frac{3}{8}$

Divisor = ________

7. $\frac{5}{7} = \frac{30}{42}$

Multiplier = ________

8. $\frac{4}{16} = \frac{1}{4}$

Divisor = ________

9. $\frac{5}{9} = \frac{25}{45}$

Multiplier = ________

10. $\frac{10}{60} = \frac{1}{6}$

Divisor = ________

11. $\frac{3}{7} = \frac{18}{42}$

Multiplier = ________

12. $\frac{24}{56} = \frac{3}{7}$

Divisor = ________

13. $\frac{5}{6} = \frac{35}{42}$

Multiplier = ________

Complete each exercise about the pairs of fraction bars.

14. What equivalent fractions are shown? ________

15. Identify the multiplier. ________

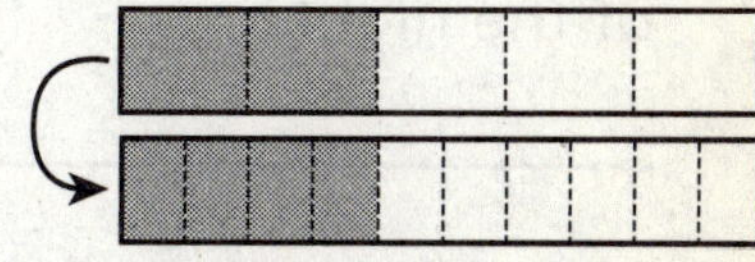

16. What equivalent fractions are shown? ________

17. Identify the divisor. ________

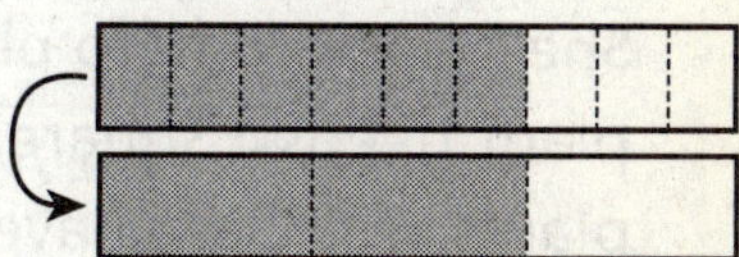

18. Write a chain with at least six equivalent fractions.

________ = ________ = ________ = ________ = ________ = ________

Remembering

Solve.

1. $\begin{array}{r} 1,000.98 \\ +\ \ 265.03 \\ \hline \end{array}$

2. $\begin{array}{r} 100,289 \\ -\ 91,460 \\ \hline \end{array}$

3. $\begin{array}{r} 312,642 \\ +\ 89,435 \\ \hline \end{array}$

4. $\begin{array}{r} 10.651 \\ -\ \ 8.092 \\ \hline \end{array}$

5. $\begin{array}{r} 0.354 \\ +\ 9.717 \\ \hline \end{array}$

6. $\begin{array}{r} 12.603 \\ -\ 2.711 \\ \hline \end{array}$

Find the area of each triangle.

7. 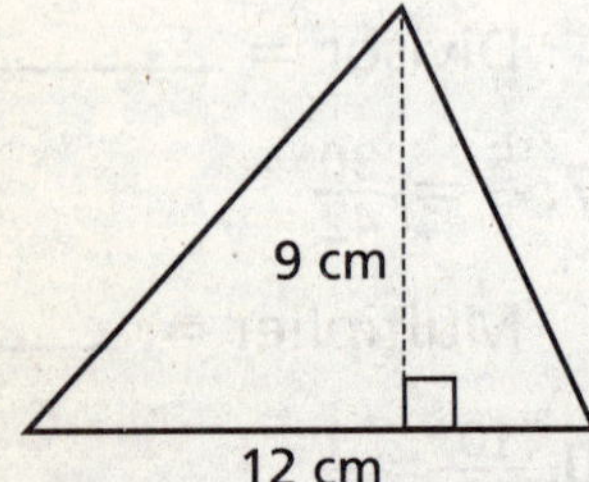

8. 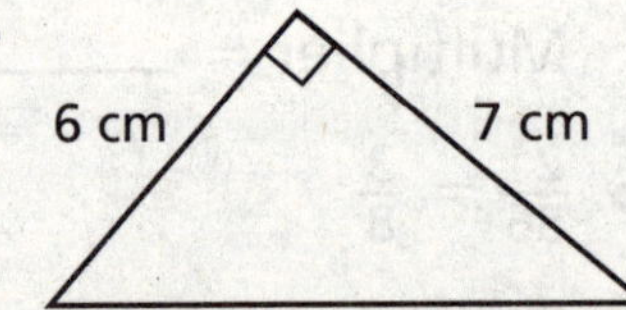

9. 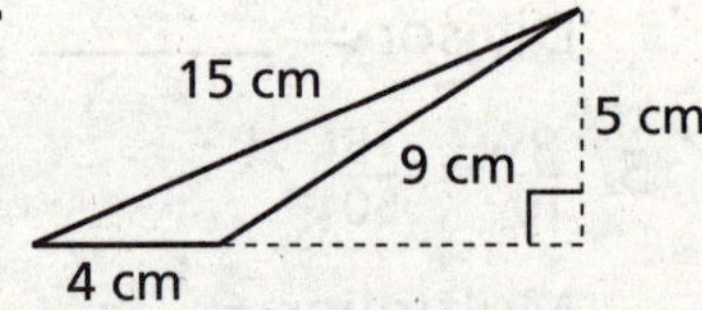

A = _____________

A = _____________

A = _____________

Solve.

Show your work.

10. A restaurant has 60 plates. One night, 9 groups of people with 6 people in each group ate dinner at the restaurant. How many plates were still clean at the end of the night?

____

11. Clara has a garden that is 7 feet wide and 4 feet long. She has 30 tomato plants to put in the garden. Each plant needs 1 square foot of space. How many leftover plants will Clara have?

____

12. Carol's bookshelf has 4 shelves with 6 books on each. Her brother Robert has 3 shelves with 7 books on each. How many books do they have altogether?

____

Equivalent Fractions and Multipliers

Name _______________________ **Date** _______________

Homework

Find _n_ or _d_.

1. $\dfrac{3}{4} = \dfrac{n}{12}$ $n =$ _______

2. $\dfrac{1}{5} = \dfrac{n}{30}$ $n =$ _______

3. $\dfrac{6}{42} = \dfrac{n}{7}$ $n =$ _______

4. $\dfrac{4}{16} = \dfrac{2}{d}$ $d =$ _______

5. $\dfrac{2}{7} = \dfrac{n}{49}$ $n =$ _______

6. $\dfrac{3}{5} = \dfrac{30}{d}$ $d =$ _______

7. $\dfrac{21}{28} = \dfrac{n}{4}$ $n =$ _______

8. $\dfrac{7}{63} = \dfrac{1}{d}$ $d =$ _______

**Answer the questions about the circle graph.
Simplify your answers.**

Rows of Garden Vegetables

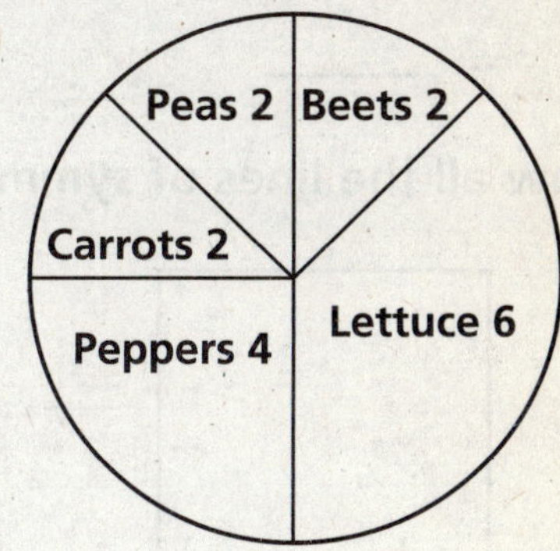

9. What fraction of the vegetables are peppers? _______

10. What fraction of the vegetables are beets? _______

11. What fraction of the vegetables are lettuce? _______

12. Arnetta planted the lettuce and the peppers.
What fraction of the vegetables did she plant? _______

**Answer the questions about the bar graph.
Simplify your answers.**

13. How many balloons are there altogether? _______

14. What fraction of the balloons are red? _______

15. What fraction of the balloons are white? _______

16. What fraction of the balloons are blue? _______

17. Estevan filled 20 balloons.
Did he fill more or less than half? _______
How do you know?

____

____

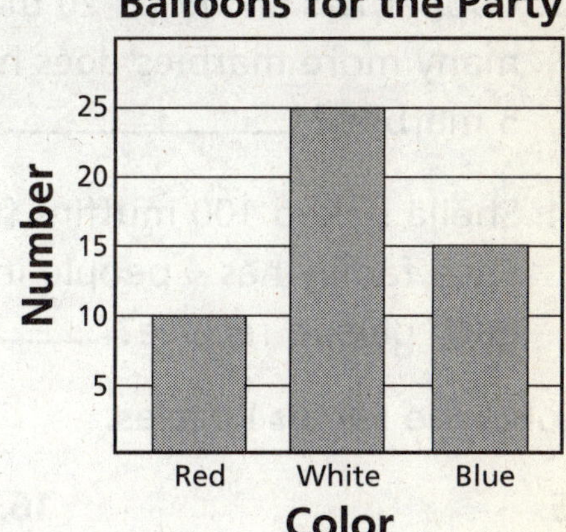

   Solve Equivalence Problems **129**

Remembering

Find the unknown number in each equation.

1. $6r + 2 = 56$

   $r =$ _______

2. $3(7 + 2) = f$

   $f =$ _______

3. $(8 \times 5) + (3 \times 7) = k$

   $k =$ _______

4. $3 + 2t = 13$

   $t =$ _______

5. $9(6 - 1) = g$

   $g =$ _______

6. $(4 \times 6) - (5 \times 2) = b$

   $b =$ _______

7. $4s - 6 = 30$

   $s =$ _______

8. $a(5 + 6) = 88$

   $a =$ _______

9. $c + (9 \times 3) = 30$

   $c =$ _______

Draw all the lines of symmetry for each figure.

10. 

11. 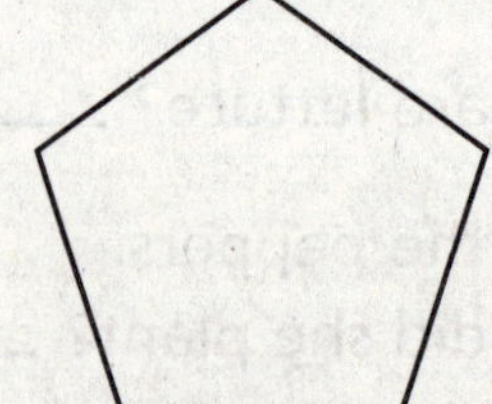

12. 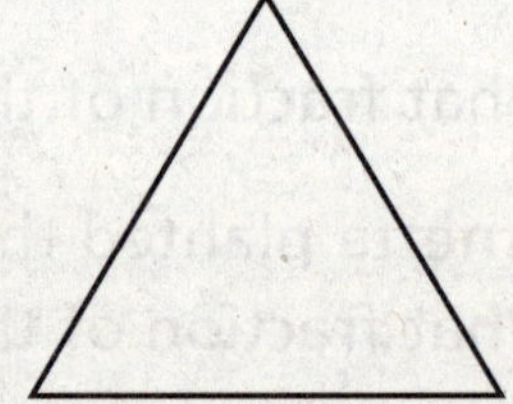

Solve each word problem.   *Show your work.*

13. Cooper has arranged 20 marbles into groups of 5. How many more marbles does he need to have 6 groups of 5 marbles? _______________________

14. Sheila baked 100 muffins for 5 families to share equally. Each family has 4 people in it. How many muffins will each person receive? _______________________

Solve the Factor Puzzles.

15. 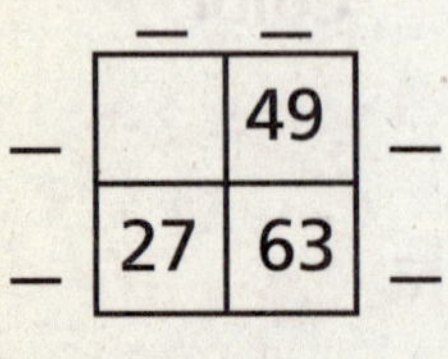

16.

30	48
	24

17.

54	48
45	

Name ___________________________ **Date** ___________________

Homework

Add or subtract.

1. $\frac{1}{3} + \frac{1}{2} =$ _______

2. $\frac{7}{10} + \frac{1}{5} =$ _______

3. $\frac{2}{9} - \frac{1}{6} =$ _______

4. $\frac{5}{32} + \frac{1}{4} =$ _______

5. $\frac{5}{6} - \frac{2}{3} =$ _______

6. $\frac{5}{11} + \frac{1}{2} =$ _______

7. $\frac{13}{16} - \frac{3}{4} =$ _______

8. $\frac{3}{7} + \frac{1}{3} =$ _______

9. $\frac{11}{12} - \frac{3}{8} =$ _______

Solve. *Show your work.*

10. Leona grew $\frac{7}{8}$ of an inch this year. Her sister Myra grew $\frac{3}{4}$ of an inch.

    Who grew more? _________________________________

    How much more? _________________________________

11. Sack A has 16 horns and 14 harmonicas. Sack B has 7 horns and 8 harmonicas. You are hoping for a harmonica.

    Which sack will you draw from? _________________

    Why? ____

    ____

12. For breakfast, Oliver drank $\frac{5}{16}$ of a pitcher of juice. His brother Joey drank $\frac{3}{8}$ of the pitcher of juice. How much did they drink together?

    ____

13. If the pitcher in exercise 12 held exactly 1 quart of juice, how much is left?

    ____

  Add and Subtract Unlike Fractions **131**

Remembering

Find the area.

1.

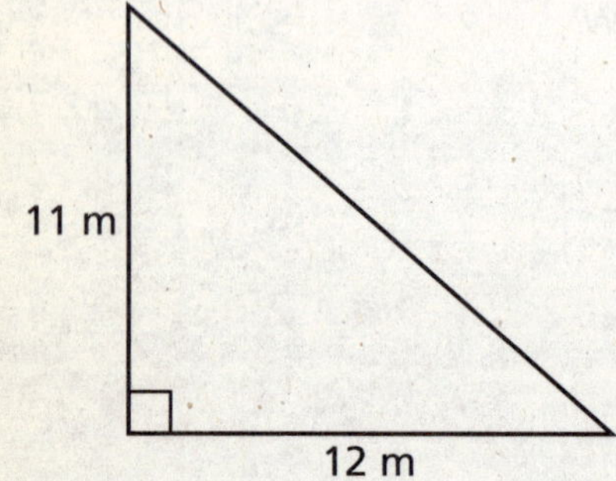

5 cm

12 cm

$A =$ _______________

2.

11 m

12 m

$A =$ _______________

Solve for n or for d.

3. $\frac{1}{6} = \frac{n}{24}$ _______

4. $\frac{3}{4} = \frac{15}{d}$ _______

5. $\frac{9}{54} = \frac{1}{d}$ _______

6. $\frac{10}{18} = \frac{n}{9}$ _______

7. $\frac{3}{7} = \frac{18}{d}$ _______

8. $\frac{3}{5} = \frac{n}{40}$ _______

9. $\frac{27}{36} = \frac{n}{4}$ _______

10. $\frac{14}{49} = \frac{2}{d}$ _______

11. $\frac{5}{6} = \frac{n}{48}$ _______

12. $\frac{1}{3} = \frac{20}{d}$ _______

13. $\frac{21}{56} = \frac{3}{d}$ _______

14. $\frac{20}{25} = \frac{n}{5}$ _______

Solve.

Show your work.

15. A truck is 5.4 m tall. It drives under a bridge that is 6.2 m tall. How much space is there between the top of the truck and the bridge?

____

16. A classroom is 10 yards long. The floor is being tiled with new square tiles that are each 10 inches long. How many tiles are needed to make one row the length of the classroom?

____

          Add and Subtract Unlike Fractions

Homework

Add or subtract. Give your answers in the simplest form.

1. $7\frac{1}{2}$
   $+\ 6\frac{5}{8}$

2. $2\frac{3}{5}$
   $+\ 5\frac{1}{4}$

3. $5\frac{3}{8}$
   $+\ 2\frac{3}{4}$

4. $3\frac{4}{15}$
   $-\ 1\frac{1}{5}$

5. $9\frac{5}{6}$
   $-\ 4\frac{1}{8}$

6. $1\frac{1}{9}$
   $+\ 3\frac{5}{8}$

7. $8\frac{1}{6}$
   $-\ 2\frac{7}{12}$

8. $6\frac{7}{9}$
   $-\ 4\frac{2}{3}$

9. $3\frac{9}{14}$
   $-\ 1\frac{2}{7}$

Solve. Give your answer in the simplest form.

Show your work.

10. Last year my elm tree was $8\frac{5}{6}$ feet tall. This year it is $10\frac{1}{12}$ feet tall. How much did it grow in one year?

11. Luis rode his bicycle $2\frac{3}{10}$ miles before lunch. He rode $1\frac{1}{4}$ miles after lunch. How far did Luis ride altogether?

12. Carrie spent $2\frac{1}{2}$ hours trimming bushes and $1\frac{1}{4}$ hours weeding the garden. She is supposed to work in the yard for 5 hours. How much longer does she need to work?

Remembering

Add or subtract. Try to do these in your head.

1. $3\frac{1}{4} + 2\frac{3}{4} =$ _______

2. $2\frac{3}{4} - \frac{1}{4} =$ _______

3. $3\frac{2}{5} + 4\frac{4}{5} =$ _______

4. $6\frac{6}{7} - 5\frac{2}{7} =$ _______

5. $8\frac{2}{3} + 1\frac{2}{3} =$ _______

6. $5\frac{6}{7} - 1\frac{2}{7} =$ _______

7. $3\frac{3}{5} + 3\frac{3}{5} =$ _______

8. $7\frac{7}{8} - 3\frac{3}{8} =$ _______

9. $5\frac{3}{8} + 3\frac{5}{8} =$ _______

Find the area and perimeter.

10. 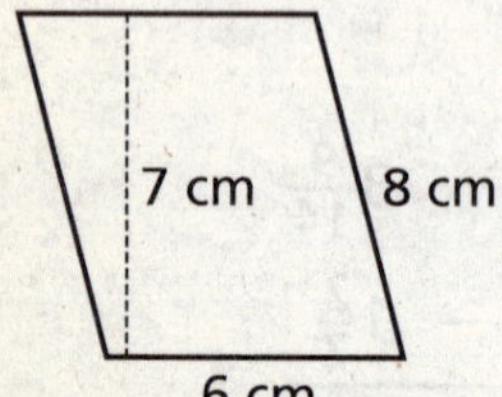

11. 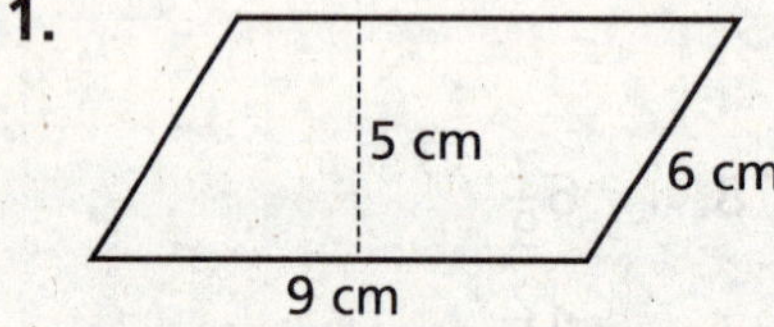

12. 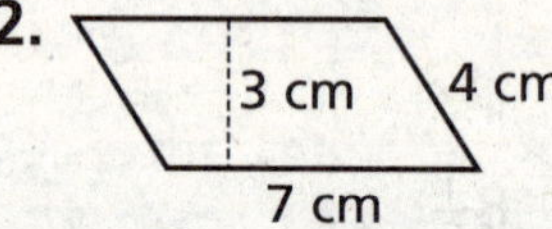

$P =$ _______

$A =$ _______

$P =$ _______

$A =$ _______

$P =$ _______

$A =$ _______

Solve the Factor Puzzles.

13.

	—	—
—	12	
—	27	45
	—	—

14.

	42
45	63

15.

18	48
	56

16.

	—	—
—		49
—	12	21
	—	—

17.

36	48
	56

18.

30	48
45	

Name _______________ Date _______________

Homework

1. Write a chain of equivalent fractions for the shaded parts of the circles below.

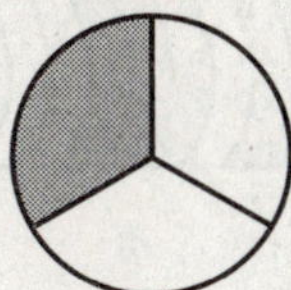 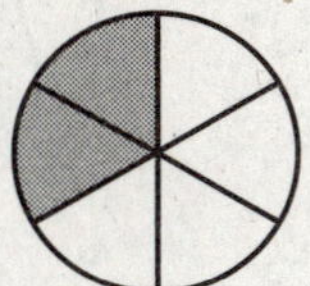 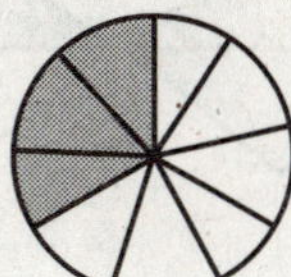 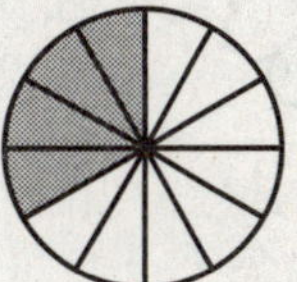 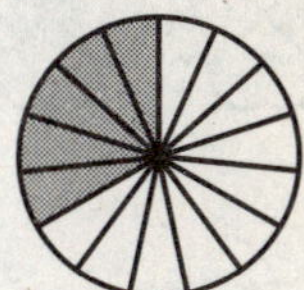

______ = ______ = ______ = ______ = ______

Add or subtract. Give your answer in the simplest form.

2. $\frac{2}{5} + \frac{1}{3} =$ ______

3. $\frac{2}{3} - \frac{1}{6} =$ ______

4. $\frac{13}{16} - \frac{3}{4} =$ ______

5. $\frac{2}{9} + \frac{1}{4} =$ ______

6. $\frac{9}{14} - \frac{2}{7} =$ ______

7. $\frac{3}{32} + \frac{3}{4} =$ ______

A gumball machine has 4 kinds of gumballs. There are 36 red ones, 24 white ones, 18 blue ones, and 12 black ones.

8. What is the total number of gumballs in the machine?

____

9. What fraction of the gumballs are red? Simplify the fraction.

____

10. What fraction of the gumballs are black? Simplify the fraction.

____

11. Pang's favorite flavors are blue and black. What is the probability that he will get one of these flavors?

Give your answer in the simplest form. ______

12. Tessa's favorite flavors are red and white. What is the probability that she will get one or the other of these flavors?

Give your answer in the simplest form. ______

13. **Challenge** Suppose Tessa put in a coin and got a red gumball. If she puts in another coin, what is the probability that she will get another red gumball? Can you simplify your answer?

____

Name ___________________ **Date** ___________________

Remembering

What mixed number is shown by each shaded part?

1.  ________

2. 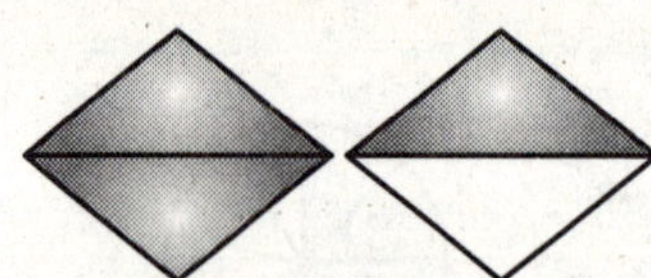 ________

3. 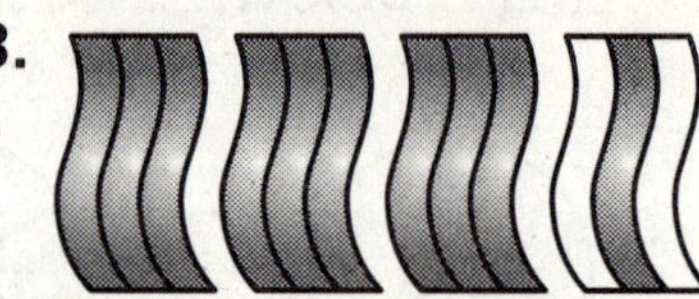 ________

Answer the questions about the bar graph. Give your answers as simple fractions.

4. How many cookies are there altogether? ________

5. What fraction of the cookies are chocolate chip? ________

6. What fraction of the cookies are oatmeal? ________

7. What fraction of the cookies are peanut butter? ________

8. Melanie baked 25 cookies. Did she bake more or less than half of the cookies? ________
How do you know? ___________________________

____

____

Which metric unit would you use to measure each item?

9. the length of your shoe ___________________

10. the length of your classroom ___________________

11. the distance across your state ___________________

12. the length of your street ___________________

13. the circumference of a dinner plate ___________________

  Practice with Unlike Mixed Numbers

Name _______________   **Date** _______________

Homework

Solve. Simplify your answers if possible.

1. What is the probability that the arrow will land on a shaded section of the spinner?

   ____

   What is the probability that the arrow will land on a white section?

   ____

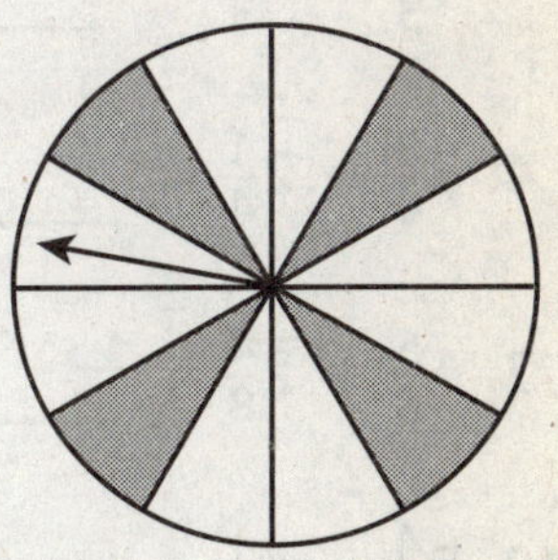

2. If you take one of these donuts from a box, what is the probability that you will get a chocolate one?

   ____

   What is the probability that you will get a vanilla one?

   ____

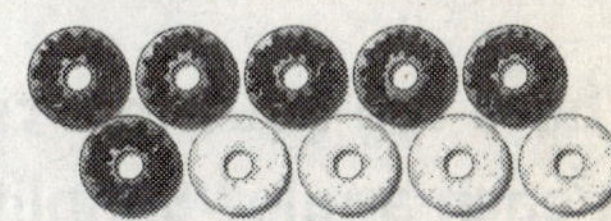

3. If you take a ring from a box with 8 silver rings and 12 gold rings, what is the probability that you will get a silver ring?

   ____

   What is the probability that you will get a gold ring?

   ____

4. This board game is called *Dungeons and Crowns*. If you land on one of the dark corner squares, you will be thrown in a dungeon. If you land on one of the squares with a star, you will be crowned monarch.

   What is the probability that you will be thrown in a dungeon?

   ____

   What is the probability that you will be crowned monarch?

   ____

Name ___________________________ **Date** ___________

Remembering

Add or subtract. Simplify. Try to do these in your head.

1. $4\frac{1}{3} + 1\frac{2}{3} =$ ______

2. $2\frac{4}{6} - 1\frac{4}{6} =$ ______

3. $3\frac{5}{10} + 1\frac{1}{10} =$ ______

4. $5\frac{3}{4} - 2\frac{1}{4} =$ ______

5. $2\frac{1}{3} + 6\frac{1}{3} =$ ______

6. $10\frac{6}{7} - 5\frac{4}{7} =$ ______

7. $1\frac{5}{8} + 2\frac{4}{8} =$ ______

8. $9\frac{4}{6} - 3\frac{2}{6} =$ ______

9. $3\frac{2}{9} + 4\frac{1}{9} =$ ______

10. $5\frac{4}{5} - 4\frac{1}{5} =$ ______

11. $3\frac{2}{8} + 5\frac{7}{8} =$ ______

12. $7\frac{3}{10} - 3\frac{2}{10} =$ ______

There are 360° in a circle. What fraction of a circle is each angle? Simplify your answers.

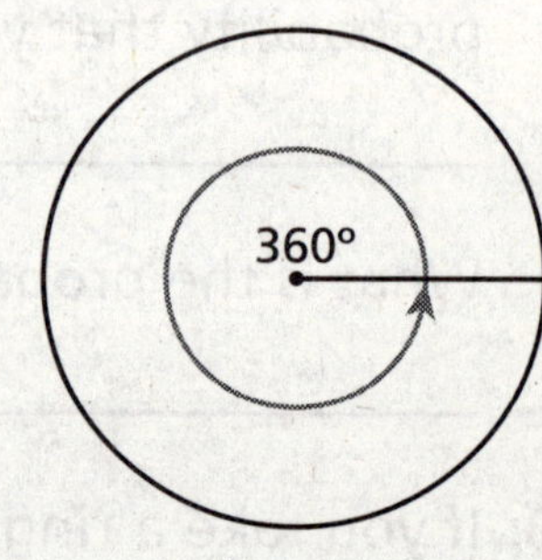

13. 90° ______

14. 45° ______

15. 180° ______

16. 120° ______

17. 60° ______

18. 30° ______

19. 10° ______

20. 5° ______

21. The 2004 population of six states is shown in the bar graph.

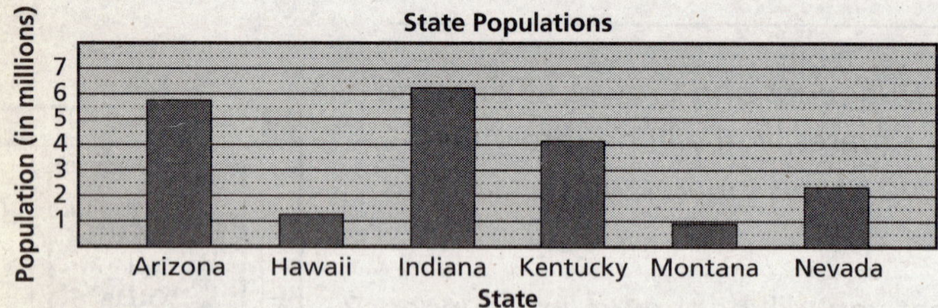

Estimate the population of each state to the nearest million.

____

____

____

    Probability and Equivalent Fractions

Homework

Match the equivalent forms.

A. $\frac{1}{2}$ **B.** 0.2   **C.** $0.\overline{3}$ **D.** $\frac{3}{4}$

1. 0.75 _______   **2.** $\frac{1}{3}$ _______   **3.** $\frac{2}{10}$ _______   **4.** 0.5 _______

**Complete the number line by writing each missing
fraction and decimal in the given boxes.**

5.

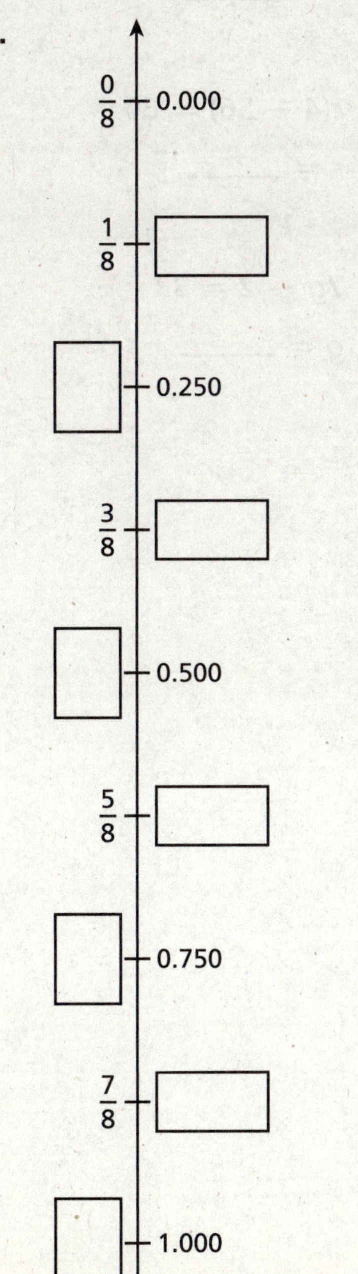

6.

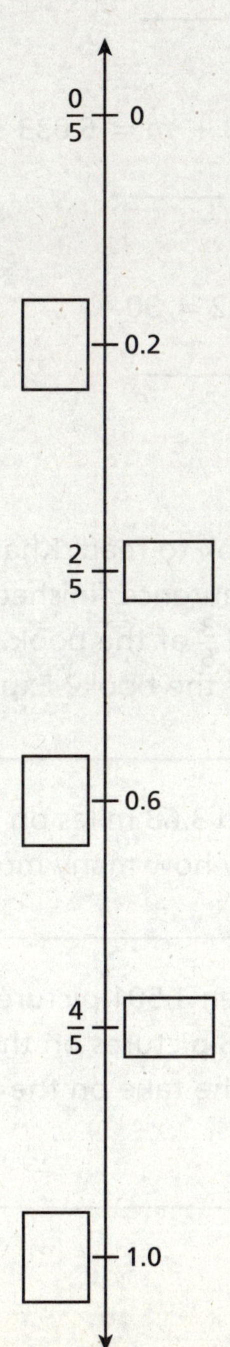

7.

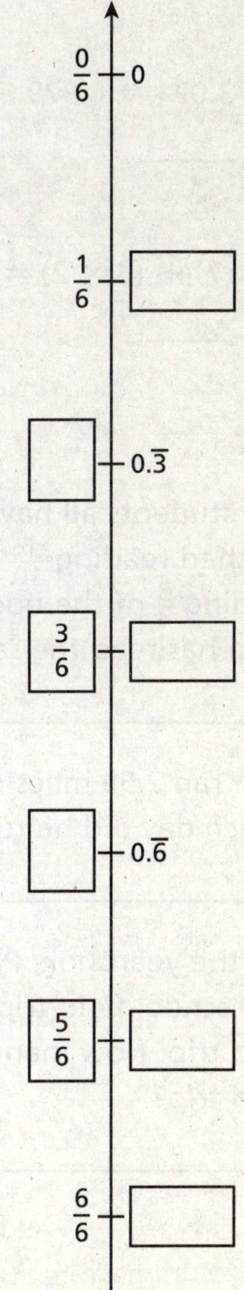

Remembering

Solve for the unknown.

1. $5.67 - 3.86 = a$

$a = $ _______

2. $11{,}402.7 - b = 1{,}889.1$

$b = $ _______

3. $14.18 + v = 15.07$

$v = $ _______

4. $n - 79.069 = 83.801$

$n = $ _______

5. $1{,}450.9 + 87.12 = e$

$e = $ _______

6. $394.621 - 206.45 = c$

$c = $ _______

7. $y - 3.021 = 6.979$

$y = $ _______

8. $4.753 + m = 6.033$

$m = $ _______

9. $r(4 + 56) = 60$

$r = $ _______

10. $(9 \times 7) + (8 \times 2) = d$

$d = $ _______

11. $7j + 2 = 30$

$j = $ _______

12. $7g - 2 = 33$

$g = $ _______

Solve.

13. The students all have the same book to read. Khalil finished reading $\frac{6}{10}$ of the book. Laurence finished reading $\frac{3}{4}$ of the book. Nahlia read $\frac{3}{5}$ of the book. Who has read the same amount of the book? Explain.

____

14. Jake ran 2.59 miles on Monday and 3.68 miles on Tuesday. Which day did he run the most? By how many more miles?

____

15. For the yearbook, Patricia had taken 1,501 pictures from two school field trips. She took 768 pictures on the first field trip. How many pictures did she take on the second field trip?

____

Fractional and Decimal Equivalencies

Homework

Compare. Write >, <, or =.

1. $\dfrac{5}{6} \bigcirc \dfrac{5}{8}$

2. $\dfrac{7}{10} \bigcirc \dfrac{9}{10}$

3. $\dfrac{8}{10} \bigcirc \dfrac{4}{5}$

4. $\dfrac{3}{4} \bigcirc \dfrac{7}{12}$

5. $2\dfrac{5}{12} \bigcirc 3\dfrac{1}{12}$

6. $4\dfrac{5}{16} \bigcirc 4\dfrac{7}{16}$

7. $21\dfrac{2}{3} \bigcirc 21\dfrac{2}{5}$

8. $5\dfrac{3}{8} \bigcirc 5\dfrac{5}{16}$

9. $6\dfrac{6}{8} \bigcirc 6\dfrac{3}{4}$

10. $\dfrac{2}{5} \bigcirc 0.4$

11. $\dfrac{1}{3} \bigcirc 0.3$

12. $0.758 \bigcirc \dfrac{3}{4}$

13. $9.58 \bigcirc 9\dfrac{7}{12}$

14. $11\dfrac{1}{8} \bigcirc 11.12$

15. $7\dfrac{5}{6} \bigcirc 7.83$

Write the numbers in order from greatest to least.

16. $\dfrac{3}{5} \quad \dfrac{3}{4} \quad 2\dfrac{4}{5} \quad \dfrac{7}{10} \quad 2\dfrac{17}{20}$ ______________________

17. $\dfrac{5}{6} \quad \dfrac{2}{3} \quad 3\dfrac{5}{9} \quad \dfrac{17}{18} \quad 3\dfrac{1}{6}$ ______________________

Write the numbers in order from least to greatest.

18. $5\dfrac{2}{3} \quad 5.6 \quad \dfrac{5}{6} \quad 0.83 \quad 5\dfrac{3}{4}$ ______________________

19. $7\dfrac{1}{2} \quad \dfrac{3}{8} \quad 0.37 \quad 7.52 \quad \dfrac{31}{4}$ ______________________

     Compare and Order Fractions and Decimals **141**

Name **Date**

Remembering

Write the measure of the unknown angle.

1.

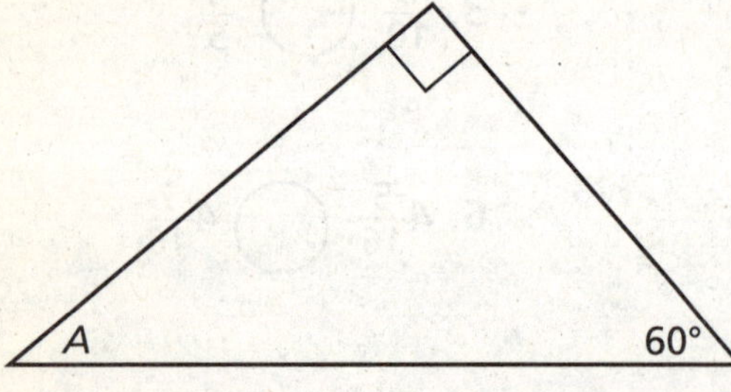

____

2.

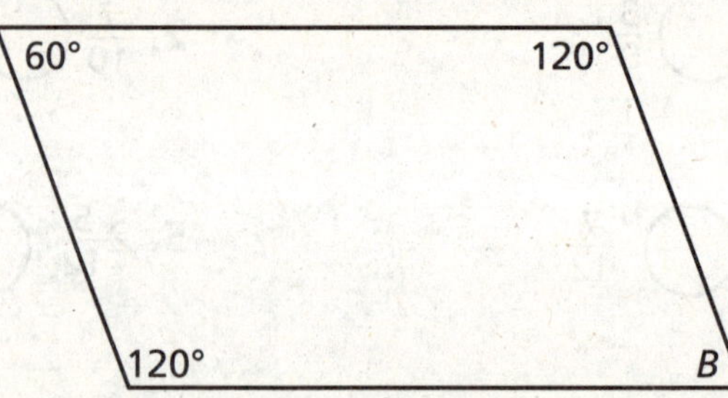

____

3.

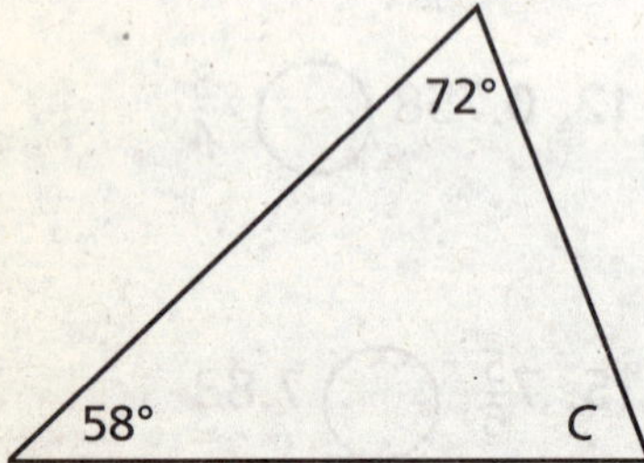

____

4.

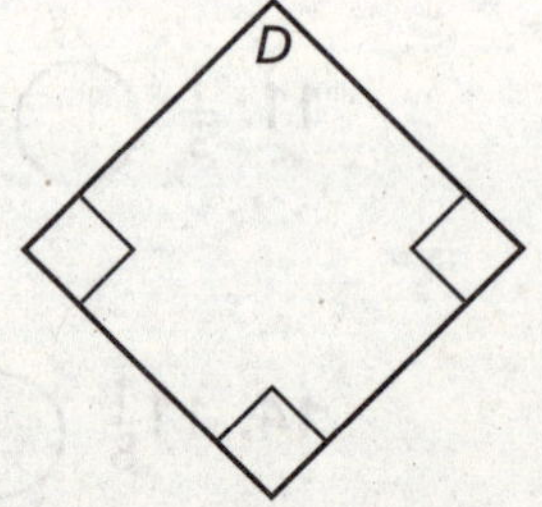

____

Solve. *Show your work.*

5. Tanya and Antoine both have a sheet of paper
that is the same size. Tanya folds her paper into eighths.
Antoine folds his paper into tenths. Who has more folds?
Who has larger folded areas?

____

6. Darren finished $\frac{5}{6}$ of his homework. Ophelia finished $\frac{1}{6}$ less
than Darren. How much of Ophelia's homework did she
finish? Simplify your answer.

____

7. A rug covers $\frac{1}{4}$ of the floor. The area of the rug is 10 ft^2.
What is the area of the floor?

____

  Compare and Order Fractions and Decimals

Name ___________________________ Date ___________

Homework

**Decide if each addend is closer to 0 or closer to 1.
Then estimate the sum or difference.**

1. $\frac{2}{5} + \frac{4}{7}$

Estimate: _______

2. $\frac{13}{20} - \frac{3}{10}$

Estimate: _______

3. $\frac{13}{18} + \frac{1}{2}$

Estimate: _______

**Estimate by rounding each number to the nearest
whole number. Then add or subtract.**

4. $3\frac{5}{8} - 1\frac{1}{2}$

Estimate: _______

5. $6\frac{4}{9} + 5\frac{7}{12}$

Estimate: _______

6. $7\frac{11}{18} - 4\frac{1}{15}$

Estimate: _______

**The list below shows the variety of flour used in four
recipes and the amounts.**

Amounts of Flour Used (lb = pound)

Flour A 4.4 lb   Flour B 5.7 lb

Flour C 5.1 lb   Flour D 4.9 lb

**Decide if each amount is closer to a whole pound or
to a half pound. Then *estimate* the total amount of
flour used.**

7. B + C _______

8. A + D _______

Solve.

9. Estimate the difference $8\frac{7}{12} - 4\frac{7}{8} - \frac{4}{10}$.
Explain how you found the answer.

____

____

Remembering

Use the diagram below to answer exercises 1–6.

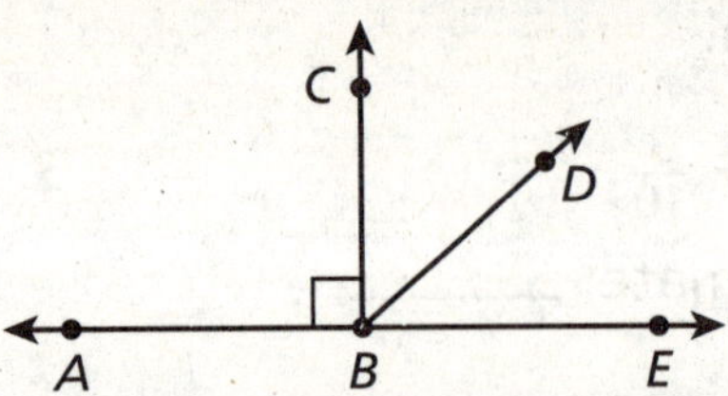

1. Which angles are complementary?

2. Which angles are supplementary?

3. Which angle is a straight angle?

4. Which angles are right angles?

5. Which angles are acute angles?

6. Which angle is an obtuse angle?

Solve.

7. Belle planted 7 marigolds in each of the 8 rows in her garden. Then she planted 2 tulips in each of the rows. If she bought 60 marigolds in all, does she have any remaining? If so, how many?

8. Lionel has three times as many DVDs as Brad. Brad has half as many DVDs as Iris. If Iris has 20 DVDs, how many DVDs do they have in all?

9. A triangle has a base of 5 cm and a height of 10 cm. A square has a side of 5 cm. Which figure has the greatest area?

Different Ways to Estimate

Name   **Date**

Homework

1. **Connections** A square rug is placed on top of a rectangular floor. The rug has a perimeter of 16 ft. The floor has a perimeter of 28 ft and a length of 6 ft. How much of the floor is not covered by the rug? Show your work.

2. **Representation** Manuel needs a length of pipe that is 0.6 ft long. He has a piece of pipe that is $\frac{3}{5}$ ft long. Does he have enough pipe? Use a number line to help you decide.

3. **Communication** Madison completed 36 out of 60 bracelets in time for the school craft fair. She says she has at least $\frac{4}{5}$ of the bracelets completed. Is this correct? Explain why or why not.

4. **Reasoning and Proof** Is it possible to draw a circle with a circumference of 30 in. inside a square with an area of 100 in.²? Explain. Draw a picture to prove your answer. Use 3 for π.

Remembering

Compare. Use >, <, or =.

1. 3,467,080 ◯ 34,670,800

2. 521,987 ◯ 521,887

3. 1,746.8 ◯ 1,746.80

4. $\frac{1}{4}$ ◯ $\frac{1}{2}$

5. $\frac{5}{6}$ ◯ $\frac{2}{3}$

6. $468\frac{1}{5}$ ◯ $4,680\frac{1}{5}$

7. $15\frac{3}{8}$ ◯ $15\frac{7}{10}$

8. $23\frac{6}{10}$ ◯ 23.5

9. $9\frac{5}{8}$ ◯ 9.62

10. $14\frac{2}{3}$ ◯ 14.68

Solve. Give your answer in the simplest form.

Show your work.

11. Tom is training for a marathon. On Monday, he walked $1\frac{3}{4}$ miles to and from a park. On Tuesday, he walked $2\frac{1}{8}$ miles to and from another park. How far did Tom walk altogether?

12. The circumference of a circle is 24 m. What is the radius of the circle? Use 3 for π.

13. A round pool has a distance of 30 ft around it. About how wide is the widest part of the pool? Use 3 for π.

Use Mathematical Processes

Homework

Solve.   *Show your work.*

1. The inside of a refrigerator is 6 feet tall, 3 feet wide, and 2 feet deep. How many cubic feet of space are inside the refrigerator?

____

2. Isabel wants to estimate the volume of her bedroom, if her bedroom was empty. Her bedroom measures 4 meters long, 3 meters wide, and 3 meters tall. What is the volume of Isabel's bedroom?

____

3. Miguel is painting letters of the alphabet on cubes. He will paint one letter of the alphabet on each face of each cube. He knows that there are 26 letters in the alphabet. How many cubes will he need if he paints each letter once? How many faces on the last cube will be empty?

____

4. How does the volume of a prism change if each dimension of the prism is doubled?

____

5. A rectangular prism has a length of 4 cm and a width of 5 cm. The volume of the prism is 200 cu cm. The height of the prism is unknown. Explain how to find the height of the prism. Then give the height.

____

____

____

Name _______________________ **Date** _______________________

Remembering

Use multiplication to write three fractions equivalent to each given fraction.

1. $\frac{2}{3}$

2. $\frac{3}{5}$

3. $\frac{5}{8}$

4. $\frac{9}{10}$

_____________   _____________   _____________   _____________

Add or subtract.

5. $\frac{2}{3} + \frac{3}{5} =$ _______________

6. $\frac{9}{10} + \frac{3}{5} =$ _______________

7. $\frac{5}{8} + \frac{9}{10} =$ _______________

8. $\frac{5}{8} + \frac{2}{3} =$ _______________

Calculate the area of each figure in square centimeters.

9.

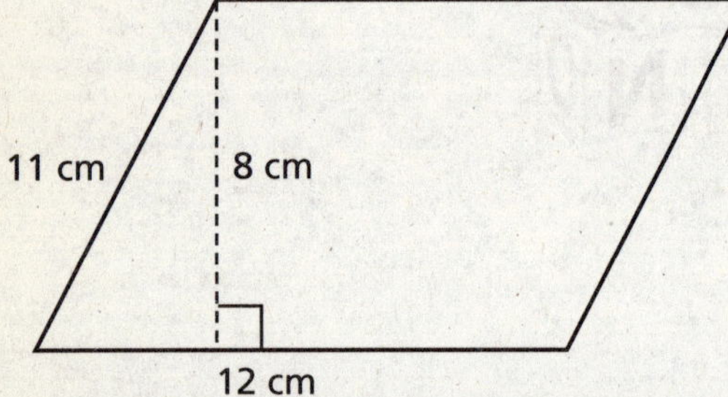

10.

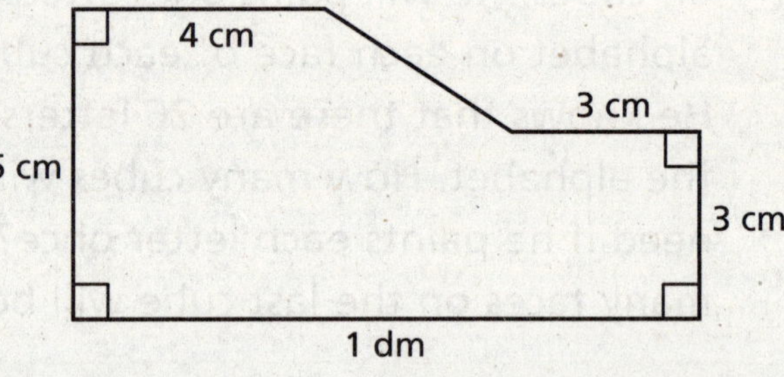

_____________________   _____________________

Draw a picture to help you solve each problem.

A right triangle has sides of 6 cm, 8 cm, and 1 dm.

11. What is its perimeter in centimeters? __________

12. What is its area in square centimeters? __________

Solve the Factor Puzzles.

13.

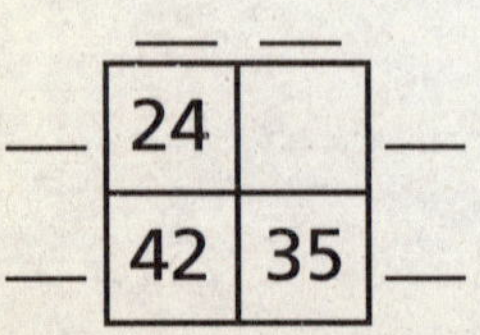

	24	
	42	35

14.

	21
72	63

15.

30	48
	40

Cubic Units and Volume

Name _______________________ **Date** _______________________

Homework

For each question, write whether you would measure for length, area, or volume.

1. The amount of space inside a moving van _______________

2. The number of tiles needed to cover a bathroom floor _______________

3. The distance from a porch to a tree _______________

4. The amount of water a tank holds _______________

5. The height of a flagpole _______________

Solve.

6. A box is 5 inches long, 4 inches wide, and 1 inch deep. How much space is inside the box?

   ____

7. Aponi built a toy chest for her niece. It has a volume of 12 cubic feet. The chest is 3 feet long and 2 feet wide. How deep is it?

   ____

8. The rug in Alan's room has an area of 18 square feet. He is planning to buy another rug that is twice as long and twice as wide. What is the area of the new rug?

   ____

9. Each drawer in Monique's nightstand has a volume of 6 cubic decimeters. Each drawer in her dresser is twice as long, twice as wide, and twice as deep. What is the volume of one of Monique's dresser drawers?

   ____

10. Fong and Daphne built these structures. Who used more cubes? How many more?

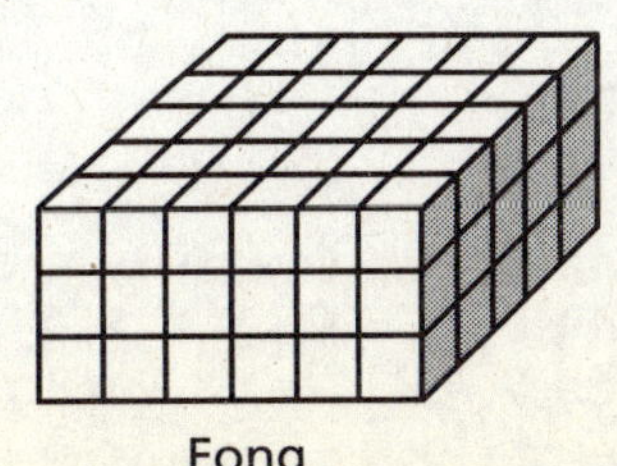

Fong

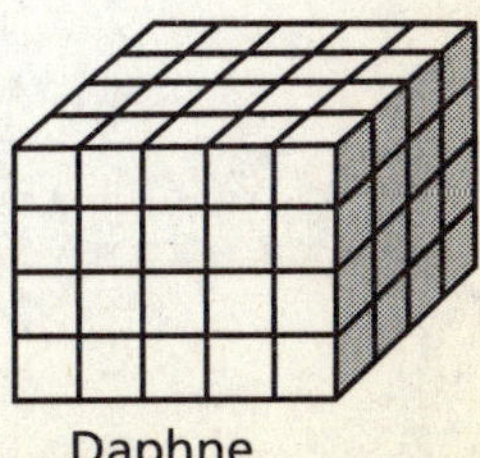

Daphne

Remembering

1. List the leaves in order from the longest to the shortest.

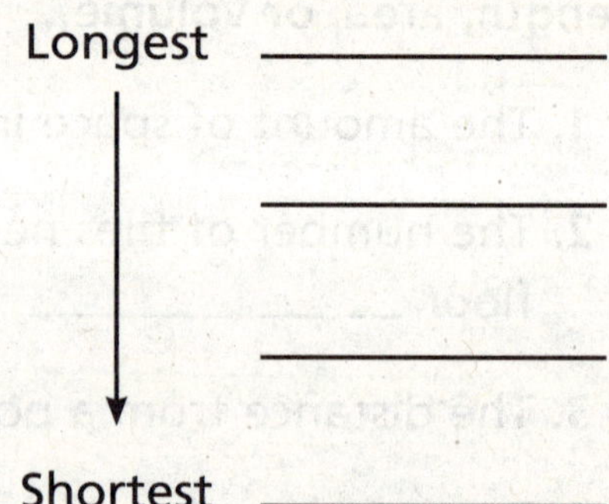

Longest _____________

Shortest _____________

Add. Write the answer as a decimal and as a fraction.

	Decimal	Fraction
2. 0.8 + 0.09	_____________	_____________
3. 0.32 + 0.4	_____________	_____________
4. 0.51 + 0.07	_____________	_____________
5. 0.006 + 0.2	_____________	_____________
6. 0.409 + 0.5	_____________	_____________

Name   **Date**

Homework

Solve.

1. 3 kL = _______ L

2. 2,500 mL = _______ L

3. 5,000 L = _______ kL

4. 1.5 L = _______ mL

5. 12 kL = _______ L

6. 7,500 mL = _______ L

7. 2 pt = _______ qt

8. 4 qt = _______ gal

9. 2 c = _______ pt

10. 3 qt = _______ pt

11. 1 qt = _______ c

12. 5 gal = _______ qt

Write a fraction.

13. What fraction of 1 gallon is 1 quart?

____

14. What fraction of 1 liter is 1 milliliter?

____

15. What fraction of 1 kiloliter is 1 liter?

____

16. What fraction of 1 pint is 1 cup?

____

Solve.   *Show your work.*

17. Cesar bought 2 bags of flour that each weighed a kilogram and another bag that weighed 500 grams. How many grams of flour did he buy?

____

18. Samantha saw two bottles of ketchup at the store for the same price. One bottle contained a liter of ketchup, and the other contained 750 milliliters of ketchup. Which bottle was the better bargain?

____

19. A pitcher is full of lemonade. Which unit of capacity best describes the amount of lemonade in the pitcher? Explain.

____

____

____

Name **Date**

Remembering

What is the area of each figure?

1. 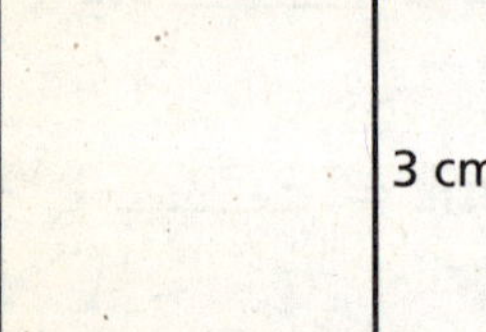

2. 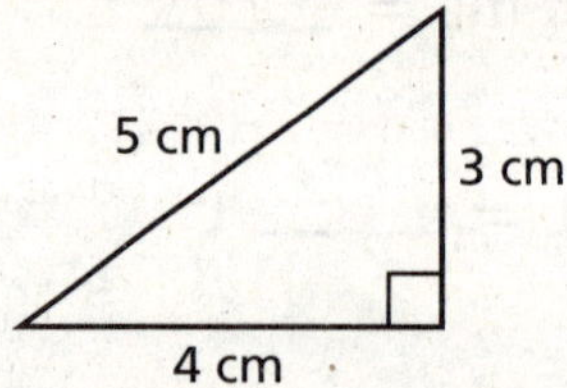

3. 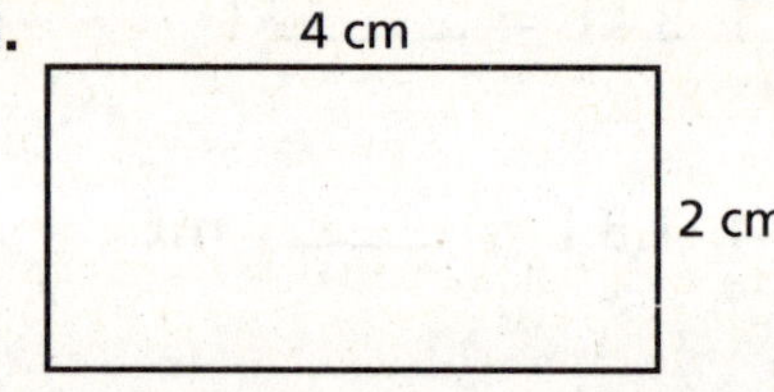

_______________   _______________   _______________

4. Look again at the figures above. Which figure has the greatest perimeter?

____

Solve. Write your answers in simplest form.

5. What fraction of 1 foot is 2 inches?

____

6. What fraction of 1 yard is 18 inches?

____

For exercise 7, write fractions in simplest form.

7. A paper bag contains 12 marbles. The marbles are identical, except for color. The bag contains 5 red marbles, 4 white marbles, and 3 blue marbles.

   What is the probability of reaching into the bag and without looking, choosing:

   a white marble?

   ____

   a blue marble?

   ____

   a red marble or a white marble?

   ____

   a marble that is not white?

   ____

   a red marble, a white marble, or a blue marble?

   ____

Homework

Complete.

1. 3 g = _____ mg

2. 50 kg = _____ g

3. 2,000 mg = _____ g

4. 2 kg = _____ g

5. 1,500 mg = _____ g

6. 7,500 g = _____ kg

7. 1 lb = _____ oz

8. 2 T = _____ lb

9. 32 oz = _____ lb

10. 1,000 lb = _____ T

11. 4 lb = _____ oz

12. 10,000 lb = _____ T

Write a mixed number in simplest form to represent each number of ounces.

13. 40 oz = _____ lb

14. 50 oz = _____ lb

15. 44 oz = _____ lb

16. 68 oz = _____ lb

17. 22 oz = _____ lb

18. 94 oz = _____ lb

Solve.

Show your work.

19. At a garden center, grass seed sells for $8 per pound. Kalil spent $10 on grass seed. What amount of seed did he buy?

20. Irina estimates that she is carrying 3 kg in her book bag. If her lunch has a mass of 500 g, what is the mass of everything else in her book bag?

21. A pickup truck is carrying 500 pounds of cargo. When empty, the truck weighs $2\frac{1}{2}$ tons. What is the weight of the truck and its cargo in tons?

22. At a grocery store, salted peanuts in the shell cost 30¢ per ounce. Is $5.00 enough money to buy 1 pound of peanuts? If it is, what amount of money will be left over?

Name ___________ **Date** ___________

Remembering

Draw and label each figure. Use your ruler or protractor.

1. ray *AB*

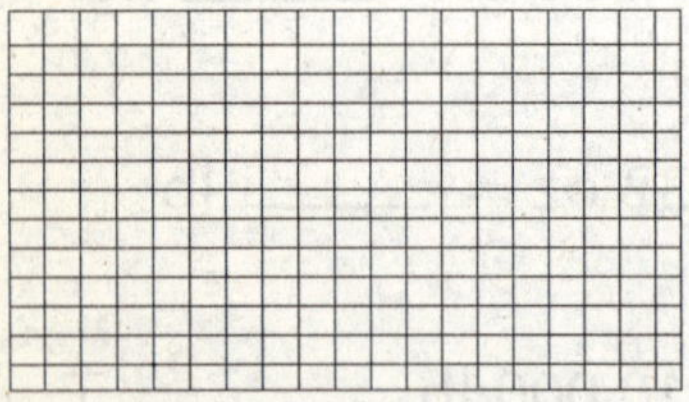

2. line segment *YN*

3. perpendicular lines *CQ* and *DX*

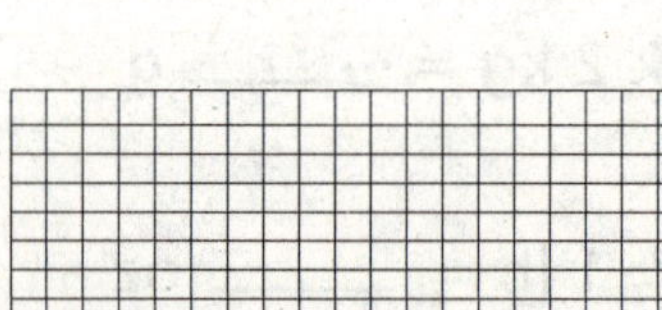

Find each missing angle measure.

4. 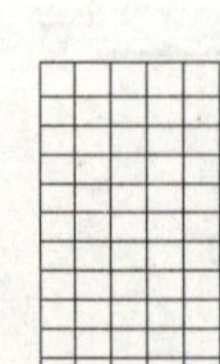

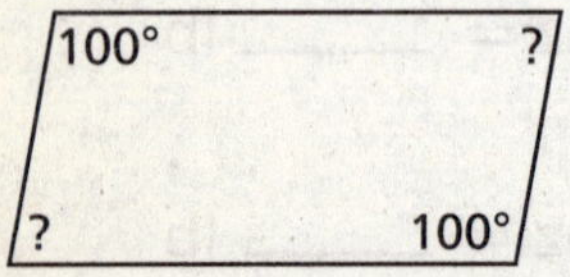

____

5. 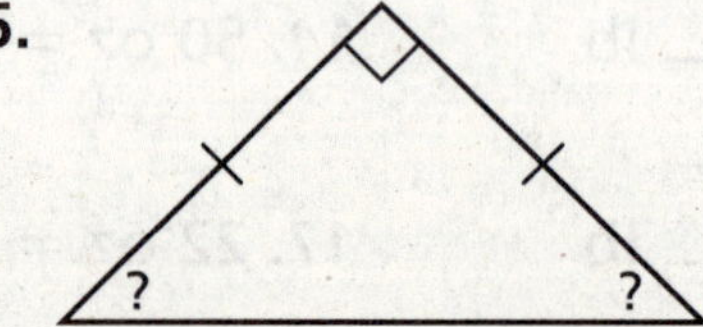

____

Compare. Write >, <, or =.

6. 27 ◯ 31

7. 54 ◯ 80

8. 106 ◯ 101

9. 330 ◯ 303

10. $\frac{1}{2}$ ◯ $\frac{5}{10}$

11. $\frac{1}{3}$ ◯ $\frac{2}{3}$

12. $\frac{7}{8}$ ◯ $\frac{3}{8}$

13. $\frac{1}{1}$ ◯ $\frac{3}{3}$

14. $\frac{3}{4}$ ◯ $\frac{7}{8}$

15. $\frac{3}{15}$ ◯ $\frac{1}{5}$

16. $\frac{5}{6}$ ◯ $\frac{1}{2}$

17. $\frac{1}{4}$ ◯ $\frac{1}{3}$

Solve.

18. Three eighths of the interior of a figure is shaded.
What fraction of the interior of the figure is not shaded?

____

Measures of Mass and Weight

Homework

Use the information in the table to complete the exercises below.

Metric	Customary
kilo = 1,000	1 pint (pt) = 2 cups (c)
milli = $\frac{1}{1,000}$	1 quart (qt) = 2 pints
	1 gallon (gal) = 4 quarts
1 gram (g) = 1,000 milligrams (mg)	1 pound (lb) = 16 ounces (oz)
1 kiloliter (kL) = 1,000 liters (L)	1 ton (T) = 2,000 pounds

1. 12 pt = _______ gal _______ qt

2. 2 L 5 mL = _______ mL

3. 2 lb 4 oz = _______ oz

4. 2,500 L = _______ kL _______ L

5. 2 kg 100 g = _______ g

6. 2 gal 1 pt = _______ c

7. 95 oz = _______ lb _______ oz

8. 3,675 mg = _______ g _______ mg

Add or subtract.

9.   4 qt 1 pt
   + 3 qt 1 pt

10.   4 pt
   − 2 pt 1 c

11.   6 gal 3 qt
   + 4 gal 2 qt

12.   13 g
   − 10 g 700 mg

13.   7 T 1,200 lb
   + 4 T   800 lb

14.   18 lb   3 oz
   − 17 lb 14 oz

15.   6 g   550 mg
   + 2 g 1,850 mg

16.   15 kL 750 L
   + 14 kL 250 L

17.   13 gal 1 qt
   −   9 gal 2 qt

Name ___________________________ **Date** ___________________________

Remembering

Find *n* or *d*.

1. $\dfrac{3}{10} = \dfrac{n}{90}$ $n =$ _______

2. $\dfrac{4}{9} = \dfrac{36}{d}$ $d =$ _______

3. $\dfrac{6}{8} = \dfrac{3}{d}$ $d =$ _______

4. $\dfrac{24}{56} = \dfrac{n}{7}$ $n =$ _______

5. $\dfrac{35}{45} = \dfrac{n}{9}$ $n =$ _______

6. $\dfrac{6}{7} = \dfrac{54}{d}$ $d =$ _______

Add or subtract. Give your answers in the simplest form.

7. $7\dfrac{2}{3} - 5\dfrac{1}{6}$

8. $9\dfrac{3}{4} + 7\dfrac{3}{8}$

9. $2\dfrac{3}{7} + 1\dfrac{1}{2}$

10. $7\dfrac{3}{4} - 3\dfrac{5}{6}$

11. $4\dfrac{3}{5} + 2\dfrac{1}{2}$

12. $6 - 1\dfrac{7}{10}$

13. $5\dfrac{2}{3} - 3\dfrac{6}{7}$

14. $6\dfrac{2}{3} + 5\dfrac{5}{8}$

15. $8\dfrac{5}{6} + 1\dfrac{5}{12}$

Solve. Give your answer in the simplest form.

16. Out of 3 whole pizzas, $1\dfrac{7}{10}$ pizzas were eaten. How much pizza is left?

____

17. Francesca has $\dfrac{16}{7}$ ft of string for her kite. Jason has $2\dfrac{3}{4}$ ft of string for his kite. Katie has more string than either Francesca or Jason. How much string could Katie have? Explain your answer.

____

Homework

1. Ice is forming outside. What temperature in degrees Fahrenheit can it not be? in degrees Celsius?

   ____

2. Give the related temperature.

   5°C is related to _______ °F.　　86°F is related to _______ °C.

3. The temperature in the morning was 18°C. By noon, the temperature had risen 13°. What was the temperature at noon?

   ____

4. The low temperature of the day was –7°F. The high temperature of the day was 12° higher. What was the high temperature of the day?

   ____

5. The 10 P.M. temperature was 6°C. The 10 A.M. temperature was –2°C. How many degrees did the temperature change from 10 P.M. to 10 A.M.? Was the change an increase or a decrease?

   ____

6. What tools and units can be used to measure the weight and the mass of a book? Explain.

   ____

   ____

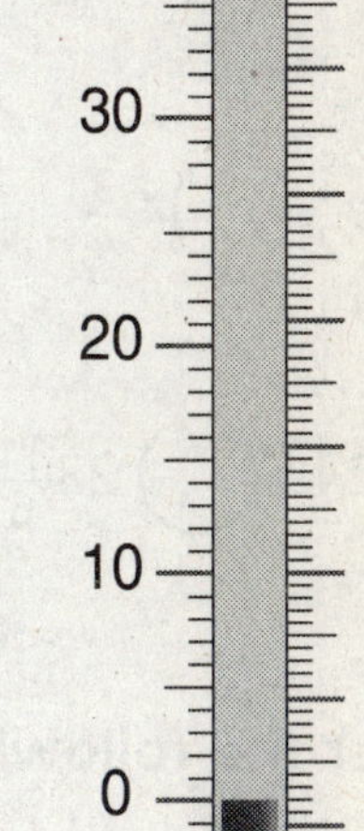
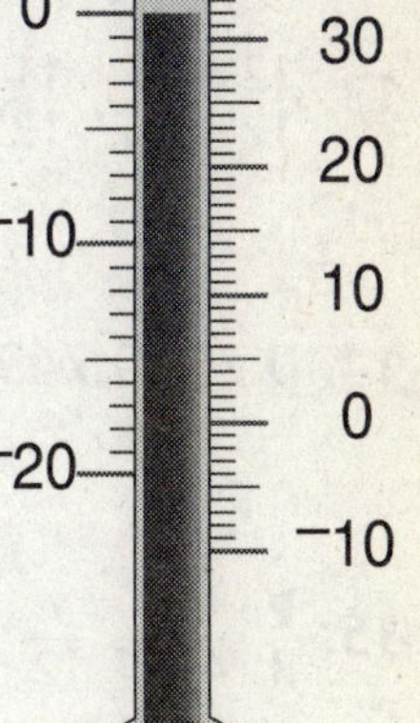

The stem-and-leaf plot shows hourly morning temperatures. Use it to answer each question.

7. How many of the temperatures are above freezing?

   ____

8. How many of the temperatures are warmer than 15°F?

   ____

Hourly Temperatures (°F)	
Stem	Leaf
0	5
1	0 4 6
2	3

Legend: 1|0 means 10°F.

Remembering

Compare. Write >, <, or =.

1. $\frac{70}{70}$ ◯ 1

2. $\frac{4}{9}$ ◯ $\frac{8}{9}$

3. $\frac{5}{6}$ ◯ $\frac{8}{9}$

4. $6\frac{13}{13}$ ◯ 7

5. $4\frac{7}{10}$ ◯ $3\frac{9}{10}$

6. $14\frac{6}{7}$ ◯ $14\frac{3}{7}$

7. $9\frac{1}{2}$ ◯ $9\frac{3}{4}$

8. $12\frac{4}{5}$ ◯ $12\frac{2}{3}$

9. $9\frac{2}{5}$ ◯ $8\frac{9}{5}$

10. $24\frac{1}{3}$ ◯ $23\frac{11}{6}$

11. $4\frac{5}{6}$ ◯ $4\frac{3}{4}$

12. $3\frac{2}{3}$ ◯ $2\frac{7}{4}$

Order the following from least to greatest.

13. $\frac{12}{12}$, $1\frac{5}{12}$, $\frac{11}{12}$, $1\frac{1}{12}$, $\frac{19}{12}$

____

14. 0.75, 0.749, 0.7, 0.707

____

15. $\frac{2}{3}$, $\frac{1}{4}$, $\frac{1}{6}$, $\frac{7}{12}$

____

Solve.

16. Karla is choosing a writing tool from Box A with 12 pencils and 8 pens. Pablo is choosing a writing tool from Box B with 7 pencils and 3 pens. Who has the better chance of choosing the pencil? Why?

____

____

Homework

Complete.

1. $1\frac{1}{2}$ days = _______ hours

2. 5 min 27 sec = _______ sec

3. 28 months = _______ years
_______ months

4. $1\frac{1}{2}$ hr = _______ min

5. 49 hr = _______ days _______ hour

6. 248 min = _______ hr _______ min

7. 28 days = _______ weeks

8. $3\frac{1}{4}$ min = _______ sec

Solve.

9. It takes Dan 25 minutes to walk to work. If he arrived at work at 6:40 A.M., when did he leave his house?

10. Soccer practice is 2 hours 10 minutes long. What time did practice start if it ended at 1:05 P.M.?

11. Karolinka went to sleep at 9:45 P.M. and awoke at 6:30 A.M. How long did Karolinka sleep?

12. The movie started at 11:35 A.M. and was 2 hours 25 minutes long. What time did the movie end?

13. Sara gave a presentation at the Science Fair from 8:12 A.M. through 11:02 A.M. Between those times, a 35-minute lunch was given. What was the actual length of Sara's presentation?

14. On Saturday, Colby studied from 10:35 A.M. to 11:30 A.M., from 11:55 A.M. to 2:30 P.M., and from 3:15 P.M. to 5:40 P.M. What is a reasonable estimate of the length of time he studied on Saturday?

Remembering

Compare. Write >, <, or =.

1. 0.4 ◯ 0.40

2. 0.7 ◯ 0.07

3. 0.54 ◯ 0.543

4. 1.6 ◯ 1.599

5. 32.853 ◯ 32.851

6. 0.8 ◯ $\frac{4}{5}$

7. $\frac{1}{4}$ ◯ 0.26

8. $\frac{9}{10}$ ◯ 0.899

9. $23\frac{2}{5}$ ◯ 23.41

10. $10\frac{1}{2}$ ◯ 10.52

11. 5.3 ◯ $5\frac{3}{4}$

12. 66.2 ◯ $65\frac{6}{5}$

Order the following from greatest to least.

13. $3\frac{1}{6}$, $2\frac{5}{3}$, $3\frac{5}{8}$, $3\frac{3}{4}$ _________________

14. 0.5, $\frac{5}{6}$, 0.7, $\frac{2}{3}$ _________________

15. $4\frac{3}{5}$, 4.1, $4\frac{1}{2}$, 4.2 _________________

Solve. Use 3 for π.

16. The circumference of a circle is 18 ft. About how long is the diameter of the circle?

____

17. Circle A has a circumference of 24 m. Circle B has a radius of 5 m. Which circle has the greater circumference?

____

The Passing of Time